Beginner's Self-Study Course Spanish

Study Guide

María Engracia López Sánchez

In collaboration with
Dominique Nißler

BARRON'S

First edition for the United States and Canada published in 2006 by
Barron's Educational Series, Inc.

All inquiries should be addressed to:
Barron's Educational Series, Inc.
250 Wireless Boulevard
Hauppauge, NY 11788
http://www.barronseduc.com

ISBN-13: 978-0-7641-3336-7
ISBN-10: 0-7641-3336-5
Library of Congress Control Number 2005908543

Printed in China
9 8 7 6 5 4 3

Welcome to the world of Spanish language

You want to learn Spanish quickly, and you're enthusiastic and motivated? You're interested in learning how to handle everyday situations and enjoy a vacation in Spain or Latin America? This course will help you learn to communicate successfully during your visit and master everyday words and phrases. Using a modern, communicative approach to language learning, you can practice speaking and understanding in real-life situations. A compelling story line that runs throughout the book provides a focus on authentic, colloquial Spanish. At the same time, a variety of exercises will help you acquire a solid foundation in basic grammar and vocabulary, geography, history, and overall culture. Because the design of the course is so flexible, it can be used both by beginners and by those who want to refresh their skills. Intelligent feedback and helpful tips on language learning enable you to learn the language at a faster pace and on your own.

How is the course structured?

The course consists of sixteen lessons and four reviews. After every four lessons, the material presented is repeated in one of the review sections.

Each lesson covers four areas:

▶ Getting Started Here we'll prepare you for the dialogue and the contents of the lesson.

▶ For Your Ear The focus here is on the dialogue or the story installment. You'll practice understanding colloquial speech and pronouncing Spanish correctly.

▶ For Practice The content — grammar, communication, or vocabulary — is presented systematically. Then, a variety of exercises will prove that practice makes perfect.

▶ In Conclusion Intercultural tips, games, or additional exercises round out and reinforce the lesson.

The reviews are also divided into four areas:

▶ Communication Here you'll find drills to help you practice the material presented in the previous four lessons.

▶ Grammar This section contains exercises that repeat the most important points of grammar.

▶ Vocabulary Here you have an opportunity to repeat the recently introduced vocabulary items once more.

▶ Pronunciation Here you can practice your pronunciation again, in detail.

By looking at the top of the page, you can easily tell in what area you're at that moment. In addition, you'll find information about the contents of the page you're on.

Exercises:

The exercises are numbered consecutively throughout the lessons, so that you can quickly get an overall idea of where you are. In addition, the numbering will be helpful when you need to check your answers. You'll find the correct answers in the companion book. Little icons will indicate whether you need a pencil, an additional sheet of paper, or one of the CDs for each exercise:

1
TR. 01 This icon shows which CD you need for this exercise: The top number tells you which of the audio CDs you need, while the bottom number refers to its track.

 For an exercise with this symbol, you need a pen or pencil to write something down or fill in a blank.

▼

For these exercises, too, you need a pen or pencil, but only to mark a correct answer or to draw a line connecting items.

This icon lets you know that you'll need an additional sheet of paper to do the exercise.

This symbol encourages you to pay close attention to the contents.

Good to know:
Remember that **mí** needs a written accent mark to distinguish it from **mi** (*my*).

In the box, you will find useful, interesting information about the Spanish language and cultural characteristics.

The vocabulary box contains words and expressions that are helpful in doing the exercises.

◄ **una señora activa** —
an active lady
tímido/a —
shy, timid

▶ **§ 1 The Alphabet**   These grammar references tell you where to find additional information on a particular aspect of grammar.

Table of Contents:

To get a quick overview of the course and the subject matter, you can look things up in two different tables of contents:

Table of Contents, Arranged by Lesson:
Here you see what material is contained in the individual lessons and reviews.

Table of Contents, Arranged by Category:
This table of contents is divided into various categories: *Dialogues, Communication, Grammar, Vocabulary, Pronunciation,* and *Intercultural Tips.*

If you want to study or review a certain topic, you can quickly find out here what exercises you need to work on for that purpose.

Companion Book:

This book contains the following:

Transcriptions:
Everything you hear on the CD you can find here in print as well. And if you didn't quite understand the dialogues, you will find the translations here helpful.

Answers:
So that you know what you got right and what you didn't, the correct answers for all the exercises are provided here, along with intelligent feedback and tips to help you learn.
Tip

Grammar Overview:
Would you like to look something up? Here you'll find thorough explanations of all the important points of grammar covered in this course.

Word List:
In this alphabetically arranged list of words, you can quickly find all the words used in this course, along with their translations.

Audio-CDs:

The set includes:
· Two audio CDs with all the sound files and dialogues.
· One audio CD with a vocabulary coach. Here you can listen to all the words and expressions, and you'll have a chance to practice vocabulary items and pronunciation.
· One audio CD for the road. A CD containing the complete serialized story, as well as selected sentences for practice. With this CD, you can learn and practice Spanish wherever you are, and thus you can master the language at a faster pace.

1 *Saying hello • Introducing yourself • Pronunciation • Nouns • Articles*

Getting Started: Spanish-speaking countries — Well-known Spanish words   **11**
For Your Ear: Rosita's arrival in the shared apartment — Saying hello and introducing yourself   **12**
For Practice: Saying hello and introducing yourself — Pronunciation — Nouns — Articles — The verb **ser**   **14**
In Conclusion: Numbers from 0 to 9 — Intercultural tip: A kiss or a handshake when saying hello?   **18**

2 *Looking at the apartment • Stress • Adjectives • Regular verbs ending in -ar*

Getting Started: Rooms of the house and furnishings   **19**
For Your Ear: Chema shows Rosita the apartment — The pronunciation of **r**   **20**
For Practice: Stress — Adjectives — Regular verbs ending in **-ar** — Negations — Numbers from 10 to 19   **22**
In Conclusion: Languages in Spain — Intercultural tip: Madrid   **26**

3 *Getting acquainted • Reflexive verbs • Regular verbs ending in -er • ser and estar*

Getting Started: Getting acquainted — Saying good-bye   **27**
For Your Ear: Rosita meets her neighbors   **28**
For Practice: Reflexive verbs — Regular verbs ending in **-er · ser** and **estar** — Adjectives of nationality — Occupations   **30**
In Conclusion: Role play: Getting acquainted — Intercultural tip: Mexico City   **34**

4 *The family • Regular verbs ending in -ir • Demonstratives • estar and hay • Possessives*

Getting Started: Nouns of relationship — Personal belongings   **35**
For Your Ear: Charo looks for her purse   **36**
For Practice: Regular verbs ending in **-ir** — Demonstratives — **estar** and **hay** — Possessives   **38**

In Conclusion: Numbers from 20 to 50 — Game: Bingo — Intercultural tip: Spanish names   **42**

Review 1

Communication: Questions and answers — Getting acquainted — Giving personal information   **43**
Grammar: Articles, nouns, adjectives — **ser, estar, hay** — Verbs in the present tense   **45**
Vocabulary: Personal belongings — Furniture — Nouns of relationship — Occupations — Numbers — A postcard from Mexico   **47**
Pronunciation: The pronunciation of certain sounds — Listening to a dialogue   **50**

5 *Leisure activities • The present perfect **muy** and **mucho***

Getting Started: Leisure activities — Personal characteristics   **51**
For Your Ear: Late in the evening at the Giménez apartment — Talking about leisure activities   **52**
For Practice: **muy** and **mucho** — The present perfect — Indicating the sequence of past events   **54**
In Conclusion: Numbers from 51 to 100 — Intercultural tip: **Don** and **Doña**   **58**

6 *At the market • Telling time • Making a date*

Getting Started: Fruits and vegetables — Days of the week — Statements of time   **59**
For Your Ear: Noelia shops at the market — At the market   **60**
For Practice: The irregular verbs **poner, querer, poder,** and **ir** — Telling time — Making a date — Numbers over 100   **62**
In Conclusion: Role play: At the market — Intercultural tip: Vocabulary differences   **66**

7 *Means of transportation • Giving directions • Prepositions • Times of day*

Getting Started: Means of transportation — Statements of location   **67**
For Your Ear: Rosita has a date — Giving directions   **68**

Contents   by Lesson

For Practice: The irregular verbs **conocer** and **decir** — Prepositions — Times of day — Giving directions — Stress and written accents   70
In Conclusion: Story in pictures: Giving directions — Game: Guess the letters — Intercultural tip: Spanish addresses   74

8 *Sports • Shopping • Pronouns • Colors*

Getting Started: Gift items — Sports   75
For Your Ear: Chema and Rosita buy a present for Noelia   76
For Practice: The interrogative **cuánto** — Demonstratives — The stressed indirect object pronouns — Position of pronouns — Colors   78
In Conclusion: Game: Bingo — Intercultural tip: Business hours in Spain   82

Review **2**

Communication: Giving directions — Answering questions   83
Grammar: Irregular verbs — **muy** and **mucho** — Pronouns — Prepositions — The present perfect   85
Vocabulary: Telling time — Statements of quantity, frequency, and place — Numbers — A postcard from Madrid   88
Pronunciation: Intonation — Stress and written accents   90

9 *The present participle • Eating and drinking • bien and bueno*

Getting Started: Beverages — The present participle   91
For Your Ear: Conversation between Charo and Agustín — Fixing dinner   92
For Practice: **estar** + the present participle — **bien** and **bueno** - **el mismo / la misma / lo mismo** — The use of the present perfect   95
In Conclusion: The **tortilla**   98

10 *Spanish tapas • Talking about daily life • The impersonal form se • Comparisons*

Getting Started: Spanish **tapas** — Describing the day's events   99
For Your Ear: In their favorite bar — Talking about daily life   100
For Practice: The impersonal form **se** — Comparisons — The present participle — Expressing agreement and disagreement   102
In Conclusion: Role play: A survey — Intercultural tip: **Tapas** bars   106

11 *Parts of the body • Health problems • Giving advice • Adverbs • Describing people*

Getting Started: Parts of the body — Describing physical complaints   107
For Your Ear: In the family doctor's waiting room — Giving advice   108
For Practice: Adverbs — The expression **hay que** — Stressed possessives — Describing people — Expressing wishes   110
In Conclusion: Song — Crossword puzzle   114

12 *Celebrating a birthday • At the restaurant • The preterit • Interrogatives • Relative clauses*

Getting Started: Dishes — The preterit   115
For Your Ear: Noelia's birthday — Birthday songs — Setting the table   116
For Practice: Interrogatives — Relative clauses — The preterit   118
In Conclusion: Role play: At a restaurant — Intercultural tip: At a restaurant in Spain   122

Review **3**

Communication: Reacting properly — Answering questions — Describing appearance   123
Grammar: The present participle — Relative clauses — Comparisons — **bien** and **bueno** — Verbs in the present, present perfect, and preterit — Present perfect vs. preterit   125
Vocabulary: Foods and drinks — Setting the table — Parts of the body — A postcard from Salamanca   128
Pronunciation: Elision — Describing the day's activities   130

13 *The Weather · The Imperfect · Comparisons · Diminutives*

Getting Started: The weather — Describing feelings and moods **131**
For Your Ear: Noelia comes home — Seasons and months **132**
For Practice: The ending **-ísimo** — Indefinite pronouns — Diminutives — Personal direct objects — The imperfect **134**
In Conclusion: The weather in Spain — Intercultural tip: The **movida 138**

14 *At the Mexican restaurant · Irregular forms in the preterit · Imperfect vs. preterit*

Getting Started: Mexican dishes — Expressing surprise **139**
For Your Ear: At the Mexican restaurant **140**
For Practice: Irregular forms in the preterit — Imperfect vs. preterit — Story in pictures — Expressing surprise — Mexican dishes **142**
In Conclusion: Role play — Intercultural tip: Corn **146**

15 *Stating plans and intentions · Prepositions of time*

Getting Started: Stating plans and intentions — A language school **147**
For Your Ear: Doña Amparo's secret — Stating plans and intentions **148**
For Practice: Stating plans and intentions — Placement of pronouns — **ser** and **estar** — Prepositions of time — Stressed and unstressed possessive adjectives **150**
In Conclusion: A puzzle — Intercultural tip: Spanish lotteries **154**

16 *Travel and hotel · Computer and Internet · On the telephone*

Getting Started: A trip to Mexico — Computer-related vocabulary **155**
For Your Ear: Noelia and Chema's trip — Surfing the Internet — Calling the travel agency **156**
For Practice: **seguir** + the present participle — The relative pronouns **el / la / los / las que** — The **dative of interest** — At the hotel — Using the telephone **158**
In Conclusion: A crossword puzzle — Intercultural tip: The Yucatán Peninsula **162**

Review **4**

Communication: Reacting appropriately — Describing feelings and moods — Stating plans and intentions **163**
Grammar: Preterit vs. Imperfect — Prepositions of time — Direct object pronouns — **seguir** + the present participle — **ser** and **estar 165**
Vocabulary: The months — The weather — Feelings and moods — Travel-related vocabulary — A postcard from Yucatán **167**
Pronunciation: Elision — Mexican dishes **170**

Dialogues

Rosita's Arrival in the Shared Apartment
L1 • E3, E4, E7

Chema Shows Rosita the Apartment
L2 • E3, E4, E7

Rosita Meets Her Neighbors   L3 • E3, E4, E6

Charo Looks for Her Purse   L4 • E3, E5, E6

Late in the Evening at the Giménez Apartment
L5 • E3, E4, E5

Noelia Shops at the Market   L6 • E3, E4, E6

Rosita Has a Date   L7 • E3, E5, E6

Chema and Rosita Buy a Present for Noelia
L8 • E3, E5, E6

Conversation between Charo and Agustín
L9 • E3, E5, E6

In Their Favorite Bar   L10 • E3, E5, E6

In the Family Doctor's Waiting Room
L11 • E3, E5, E6

Noelia's Birthday   L12 • E3, E4, E5

Noelia Comes Home   L13 • E3, E4, E6

At the Mexican Restaurant   L14 • E3, E4, E6

Doña Amparo's Secret   L15 • E3, E4, E6

Noelia and Chema's Trip   L16 • E3, E4, E6

Communication

Saying Hello, Introducing Yourself, and Saying
Good-bye   L1 • E8, E15   L3 • E2

Getting Acquainted   L3 • E1, E5, E16

Making a Date   L6 • E14, E15

Giving Directions   L7 • E12, E16   R2 • E2

Shopping   L6 • E5, E18   L8 • E1

In a Restaurant   L12 • E18   L14 • E5, E16

In a Hotel   L16 • E13, E14

Writing a Postcard   R1 • E20   R2 • E18
  R3 • E17   R4 • E22

Using the Telephone   L16 • E15

Expressing Surprise   L14 • E2, E14

Expressing Obligation   L6 • E9   L11 • E12

Giving Advice   L11 • E4, E7

Expressing Wishes   L11 • E16

Stating Plans and Intentions
L15 • E1, E7, E8, E9, E10

Grammar

Articles   L1 • E13   L2 • E10

Nouns   L1 • E13   L2 • E9

Adjectives   L2 • E11, E12   R1 • E9

Adverbs   L11 • E9, E10

muy and **mucho**   L5 • E7, E8   R2 • E8

bien and **bueno**   L9 • E13   R3 • E10

Comparisons   L10 • E11, E12, E13   R3 • E8

Comparisons   L13 • E8, E9

Regular Verbs in the Present Tense   L2 • E13, E14
  L3 • E10, E12   L4 • E7, E8

Irregular Verbs in the Present Tense   L1 • E14
  L3 • E11   L4 • E14   L6 • E8, E10, E11   L7 • E8
  R2 • E6, E7   L11 • E8

Reflexive Verbs   L3 • E7   L10 • E7, E8

Negation   L2 • E15, E16

The Present Perfect Tense   L5 • E9, E10, E11
  R2 • E12, E13   L9 • E15

The Preterit Tense   L12 • E2, E12, E13, E14, E15, E16
  L14 • E7, E8

The Imperfect Tense   L13 • E13, E14, E15, E16

Imperfect vs. Preterit   L14 • E9, E10, E12
  R4 • E7, E8

The Present Participle   L9 • E2, E10, E11, E12
  L10 • E14   R3 • E5, E6   L16 • E8

ser — estar — hay   L3 • E13   L4 • E10
  R1 • E10, E11, E12   L15 • E12, E13   R4 • E13

The Impersonal Form **se**   L10 • E9, E10

    R3 • E9

Pronouns   L4 • E12, E13   L5 • E15

    L8 • E11, E12, E14, E15   R2 • E9, E10   L15 • E11

Demonstratives   L4 • E9   L8 • E9, E10

Possessives   L4 • E11   L11 • E13   L15 • E16, E17

Prepositions   L7 • E10, E13   R2 • E11

Relative Clauses   L12 • E11   R3 • E7   L16 • E10

Interrogatives   L8 • E8   L12 • E9, E10

Vocabulary

Family   L4 • E1, E15   R1 • E16

Rooms of the House and Furnishings   L2 • E1, E2

R1 • E15

Daily Life   L10 • E2, E16   R3 • E19

Work and Occupation   L3 • E15   R1 • E18

Leisure Time and Sports   L5 • E1, E12   L8 • E2

Eating and Drinking   L6 • E1   L9 • E1, E17

    L10 • E1   L12 • E1, E8   R3 • E13   L14 • E1, E15

Parts of the Body and Health Problems

L11 • E1, E2   R3 • E15

Appearance   L11 • E14, E15   R3 • E4

Feelings and Moods   L13 • E2   R4 • E3, E17

Means of Transportation   L7 • E1, E17

Statements of Place   L7 • E2   R2 • E16

Colors   L8 • E17, E18

Countries, Nationalities, and Languages   L1 • E1

    L2 • E18   L3 • E14

Travel   L16 • E1, E7   R4 • E21

Computers   L16 • E2, E5, E16

Weather   L13 • E1, E18   R4 • E15, E16

Days of the Week, Months, Seasons   L6 • E2

    L13 • E7   R4 • E14

Telling Time   L6 • E12, E13   R2 • E14

Numbers   L1 • E16   L2 • E17   L4 • E16

R1 • E19   L5 • E16   L6 • E16

Pronunciation

Pronunciation of **c, z, b, v / ñ, j, ll, ch**   L1 • E10, E11

    R1 • E21

Pronunciation of **r / rr**   L2 • E5

Stress and Written Accents   L2 • E8   L7 • E15

    R2 • E20

Intercultural Tips

The Polite Pronoun or the Familiar Pronoun

    L1 • E18   L5 • E18

Spain   L2 • E19

Mexico   L3 • E17   L16 • E17

Names and Addresses   L4 • E18   L7 • E18

Eating   L9 • E18   L14 • E17

Bars and Restaurants   L10 • E17   L12 • E19

    L13 • E19

Who's who in this serialized story?

The story is set in Madrid, Spain.

Rosita, Jordi, and Chema live together there in a shared apartment:

Rosita comes from Mexico and is in Madrid because she was awarded a research fellowship at the city's Museum of Modern Art. She really enjoys her work at the museum.

Jordi is from Barcelona. Right now, he's doing an internship at a local company, and after work he enjoys sports.

Chema works in an office as a designer. He likes his neighbor, Noelia.

Here you see the Giménez family. They live next to Rosita, Jordi, and Chema:

Agustín works for an international firm as a department head. He likes his work very much.

Charo is married to Agustín. She's a housewife and is always somewhat concerned about her family.

Noelia, the daughter of Agustín and Charo, is studying business administration. She's very interested in Chema!

Nacho, Noelia's brother, lives in London, where he's studying English.

Doña Amparo is Agustín's mother. She likes going out with her friends to walk in the park or see a movie.

Spanish-speaking countries — Well-known Spanish words

1 TR. 01

You're just beginning to learn Spanish. Before the process really gets under way, you need to familiarize yourself with the countries in which Spanish is spoken. Here you see Rosita's flight route from Mexico to Spain. Spanish is spoken in both countries. Where else is it spoken?

Fill in the boxes below, using the country names in the box at right. Then listen to the CD to hear how the names of these countries are pronounced in Spanish.

Cuba
Argentina
Venezuela
Chile
Colombia
México
España

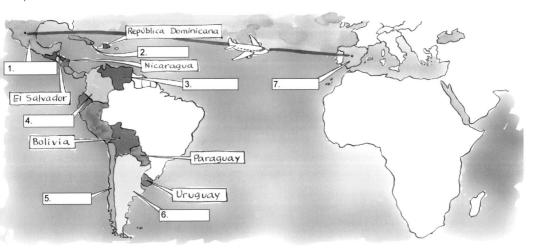

2 TR. 02

Most likely, you already know a number of words in Spanish. Look at the pictures and read the words below. Then match the words with the appropriate pictures. Next, listen to the correct answers on the CD, and pay attention to the pronunciation of the words as well.

1.   2.   3.   4.   5.   6.

_____   _____   _____   _____   _____   _____

la guitarra — el sombrero — la siesta — la paella — la sangría — la cerveza

Rosita's arrival in the shared apartment

3

In a shared apartment (**el piso compartido**) in Madrid, the doorbell rings. Chema and Jordi are getting a new apartment mate today: Rosita, from Mexico.

Listen to the dialogue on the companion CD while you look at the two pictures. The illustrations will help you understand the text.

4

Listen to the dialogue again while reading the text in the companion book. Then underline the places in the text that seem familiar or easy to you. Listen to the dialogue once more and repeat the marked words along with the speaker on the CD.

5

In which word does the indicated sound appear? Write the word in the appropriate blank, and then check your answers with the help of the CD.

> **yo** / **pla**ya — **gui**tarra — Mé**x**ico — ¡**Qué** bien! — **gue**rrilla

1. **ge** as in "get": _____   2. **gi** as in "give": _____

3. **y** as in "young": _____   4. **h** as in "house": _____

5. **ke** as in "kerosene": _____

Saying hello and introducing yourself

6 TR. 05

The dialogue contains several phrases used to greet people and make introductions. Take a close look at them now. Then listen to the following sentences on the CD, paying attention to the intonation of the questions and statements. Repeat them after the speaker. Then read the translations of the individual phrases.

1. Hola, buenos días.

2. ¿Qué tal?

3. Muy bien, gracias.

a. *Hello, good morning.*

b. *How are you?*

c. *Fine, thanks.*

4. ¿Eres catalán?

5. Yo soy Chema.

6. Éste es Jordi.

d. *Are you a Catalan?*

e. *I'm Chema.*

f. *This is Jordi.*

7. ¡Encantada!

8. ¡Mucho gusto!

g. *Delighted!*

h. *It's a pleasure!*

Good to know:
As you see, in addition to the familiar punctuation marks, Spanish also has inverted question marks and exclamation marks (¿ and ¡), which are used at the beginning of a question or an interjection.

7 TR. 03

Here you see part of the dialogue: On the left, in Spanish, and on the right, in English. Unfortunately, the English sentences are not in the right sequence. Match them with the correct Spanish sentences. If you like, at the end you can listen to the entire dialogue in Spanish again and read the full translation in the companion book.

1. *Chema:* Claro, claro. Mira, éste es Jordi.
2. *Rosita:* ¡Encantada!
3. *Jordi:* ¡Mucho gusto!
4. *Rosita:* ¿Eres catalán?
5. *Jordi:* Sí.
6. *Rosita:* ¡Qué bien! Somos un piso muy interesante.
7. *Chema:* Sí, es verdad. ¿Quieres ver el piso?
8. *Rosita:* Sí, con mucho gusto.

a. *Chema:* Yes, that's true! Do you want to see the apartment?
b. *Rosita:* Are you a Catalan?
c. *Jordi:* Yes.
d. *Rosita:* Delighted!
e. *Rosita:* Yes, I'd like to.
f. *Chema:* Of course, of course. By the way, this is Jordi.
g. *Rosita:* How nice! We're a very interesting group of apartment mates.
h. *Jordi:* It's a pleasure!

Good to know:
Jordi is a typical Catalan name, so it's easy for Rosita to guess which region of Spain he comes from.

Saying hello and introducing yourself

8

¡Hola! ¿Qué tal? is a general form of greeting. You usually answer by saying **Bien, gracias. ¿Y tú?** (familiar form). Depending on the time of day, you can also say:

> **Buenos días.** (in the morning)
> **Buenas tardes.** (after about 2 P.M. and in the early evening)
> **Buenas noches.** (after about 8 P.M.)

The pronoun **usted** is the polite form of *you* (singular; it is abbreviated in writing as **Ud.**).

 TR.06 Listen to the following short dialogues, and repeat:

> Hola, buenos días. ¿Qué tal? — Muy bien, gracias. ¿Y tú?
> *Hello, good morning. How are you? — Just fine, thanks. And you?*
>
> Hola, buenas tardes. ¿Qué tal? — Bien, gracias. ¿Y usted?
> *Hello, good afternoon/evening. How are you? — Fine, thanks. And you?*

9

In our dialogue, Chema introduces his apartment mate, Jordi. He says: **Mira, éste es Jordi.** When a woman is introduced, however, you say **ésta es** ... In response, you can say **encantado** (if you're a male) or **encantada** (if you're a female), or **mucho gusto** (invariable).

Listen to the dialogue in which Rosita, Chema, and Jordi introduce themselves. Then play the role of Rosita. What would you say in her place? Write your reactions in the blanks and say them out loud. Remember: A woman says **encantada**, a man says **encantado**.

 TR.07

Chema:	Hola, ¿qué tal?
Rosita or you:	_____
Chema:	Bien, bien. Mira, éste es Jordi.
Rosita or you:	_____
Jordi:	¡Mucho gusto!

Pronunciation

10   TR.08

Listen several times to the following words and read along. Then repeat them. Pay special attention to the pronunciation of the letters **c, z,** and **v.**

> Venezuela — gracias — cerveza

Using these examples, try to complete the following rules of pronunciation.

> I. _____ at the beginning of a word sounds like the **b** in "book"; elsewhere it is pronounced like the **v** in "level" (soft **b**, with the lips partially open).
>
> 2. _____ before **e** and **i** as well as _____ are pronounced like the **th** in "think."

Good to know:

In Latin America and southern Spain, the sound that corresponds to **th** is always pronounced like **s**. Rosita's pronunciation is an example of this. The letter **h** is always silent in Spanish, as in the word **hola.**

11   TR.09

Which of these Spanish words contains the following sounds? Match the words with the correct sounds, and check your answers with the help of the CD.

▶ § 2 Pronunciation

> mucho — español — viaje — paella

> I. _____ **gn** as in "cognac"
>
> 2. _____ **h** as in "horse"
>
> 3. _____ **y** as in "yes" or **lli** as in "million"
>
> 4. _____ **ch** as in "church"

Good to know:

The **j** in **Jordi** is not pronounced like the **j** in **viaje,** because this is a typical Catalan name. The pronunciation here resembles the **s** in "measure" or "vision."

TR.10

Do you remember the pronunciation of the word **Argentina** in the first exercise in this lesson? If not, listen carefully to it once again.
The letter **g** can be pronounced like the **j** in **viaje,** but only if it is followed by an **e** or an **i!**

Pronunciation — Nouns — Articles

12

Naturally, the pronunciation of a foreign language requires plenty of practice. Look at these five drawings, which depict new vocabulary items. Do you already know some of them? Read the words and try to say them. Then, with the help of the CD, test your pronunciation. Repeat the words several times more, so that you can master the correct pronunciation.

una cereza   una llave   una vela   un queso   una joya

13

▶ **§ 5 Nouns**

Good to know:

Nouns that end in **-ción** or **-dad** are always feminine: **la información** (*information*), **la verdad** (*truth*). Nouns that end in **-ema** are always masculine: **el tema** (*theme*).

▶ **§ 4 Articles**

Nouns in Spanish are either masculine or feminine. Usually words ending in **-o** are masculine (for example, **sombrero**). Words ending in **-a** are feminine (**fiesta**). But you have seen other examples as well, such as **viaje** (masculine) and **verdad** (feminine). In fact, there are a number of endings, and it is always best to learn a noun together with its article: **El** for masculine words and **la** for feminine words (corresponding to the English definite article, *the*).

Of course, you can also use the corresponding indefinite articles: **Un** (masculine), **una** (feminine) (English *a, an*).

TR. 12

Fill in each blank with one of the articles given, and use the CD to check your answers.

      1. ¿Quieres _____ paella?

      2. ¿Quieres ver _____ piso?   un — el — una

      3. Somos _____ piso interesante.

Which article goes with each of the following words? Mark the correct answer. For each noun, only one choice is correct.

▪ el	▪ un	▪ el	▪ la
▪ la cerveza	▪ la viaje	▪ la verdad	▪ un sombrero
▪ un	▪ una	▪ un	▪ una

*The verb **ser** — Subject pronouns*

14

The verb **ser** (*to be*) is used, for example, to indicate nationality and to give one's name, as in: **¿Eres catalán?** and **Yo soy Chema.**
On your own, carefully read the main dialogue in the companion book again, and then pick out the forms of the verb **ser** and fill in the missing forms. Then listen to all the forms on the CD and check your answers.

TR. 13

yo (*I*) _____   nosotros/nosotras (*we*) _____

tú (*you* fam.) _____   vosotros/vosotras (*you* fam.) sois

él/ella/usted   ellos/ellas/ustedes
(*he/she/you* pol.) _____   (*they/you* pol.) son

The personal pronouns are used to distinguish between various people or to emphasize them. Chema says: **Yo soy Chema,** since he is not alone (Jordi is there too). Rosita, however, says: **¡Somos un piso muy interesante!** because it's clear that she is referring to all three of them.

15 ✏

A friend in Mexico has asked Rosita to take a little present to his aunt, María Riera, who lives in Madrid. Rosita has never met her before, and she has arranged to meet her in a bar. Mrs. Riera is already sitting at a table with a friend from work, Juana, when Rosita gets there. Complete the dialogue below, in which Rosita, María, and Juana exchange greetings, by filling in the blanks with the correct words.

Rosita: ¿ _____ usted María Riera?

María: Sí.

Rosita: ¡Hola! _____ Rosita.

María: ¡Hola, Rosita! ¿ _____ ?

Rosita: Muy bien, gracias, ¿ _____ ?

María: Bien ... Mira, _____ es Juana.

Rosita: _____ .

Juana: Mucho gusto.

> qué tal — ésta — soy — encantada — es — y usted

Good to know:

There is a polite form for the singular (**usted es**) and another for the plural (**ustedes son**). The personal pronouns **nosotros** and **vosotros** also have feminine forms: **nosotras, vosotras.**

▶ **§ 25 Subject Pronouns**

Good to know:

In Latin America, **ustedes** is used in place of **vosotros:** **¿Ustedes son Chema y Jordi, ¿verdad?** instead of **¿Vosotros sois Chema y Jordi, ¿verdad?** (*You're Chema and Jordi, aren't you?*).

Good to know:

In the Spanish-speaking world, it is customary to address an older person with the polite form of *you*, but to be addressed with the familiar form in response.

Numbers from 0 to 9 — Intercultural tip: A kiss or a handshake when saying hello?

16

§ 38 Numbers

Listen to the numbers from zero to nine on the CD and repeat them. Take a look at the way the numbers are written, and then read them aloud to yourself several times, comparing your pronunciation with what you hear on the CD.

cero	uno	dos	tres	cuatro

cinco	seis	siete	ocho	nueve

17

¿Cuál es tu número de teléfono? *(What's your telephone number?).*
Listen to five short dialogues on the CD in which telephone numbers are given. Try to make out the numbers and write them down. Listen to the dialogues as often as you wish, concentrating primarily on the numbers. Then check your answers by reading the transcriptions of the dialogues in the companion book.

18

Kisses (**besos**) given when greeting someone, actually more of a brushing of cheeks, are usual in Spain (two kisses) and Latin America (one kiss) in informal situations—for example, when you are introduced by friends. Men, however, exchange kisses only in a family setting; otherwise they embrace or slap each other on the shoulder. Shaking hands is likely to be part of a very formal and professional context.

The familiar pronoun or the polite one? In Spain, people are quick to use the familiar form of *you* (**tú**), even between colleagues or in business relationships with clients. The polite form (**usted**) is a way of showing respect to older people or to superiors in a work environment. The polite form is more common in Latin America than in Spain. If you feel uncertain, start with **usted** and wait for the native speaker's reaction.

Vocabulary: Rooms of the house and furnishings

1 TR. 16

Below, you see a Spanish apartment. On the CD, listen to the Spanish words for the rooms and repeat them. Can you match the words with the right rooms? Write the numbers in the little boxes. Then look at the translations.

■ la entrada — ■ el pasillo — ■ la cocina — ■ el salón —
■ la terraza — ■ el dormitorio — ■ el baño — ■ el balcón

◀ **la entrada** –
the entrance
la terraza –
the terrace
el pasillo — *the hall*
el dormitorio —
the bedroom
la cocina —
the kitchen
el baño —
the bathroom
el salón —
the living room
el balcón —
the balcony

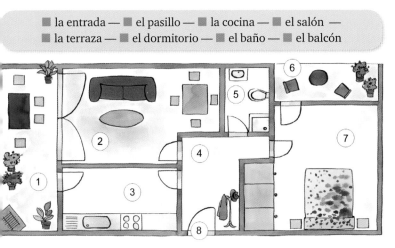

2 TR. 17

Here you see a few items found in most homes. Listen to the words on the CD and repeat them.

Good to know:
Sofá is masculine!
(<u>un</u> **sofá**)

un escritorio

un sofá

una bañera

un ordenador

un horno microondas

una alfombra

una estantería

un sillón

Which of these objects do you have in your home?
Write a list in Spanish.

*Chema shows Rosita the apartment — The pronunciation of **r***

3

Chema shows Rosita, his new apartment mate, her room and the other rooms in the apartment. Listen to the dialogue and look at the pictures below. The pictures will help make the meaning clear. Then listen to the dialogue again. If you like, you can read along, using the text in the companion book.

4

Now listen to the dialogue once more, and read along in the companion book. How do you say "You're welcome" in Spanish? Find the expression in the dialogue and write it in the balloon.

5

Good to know:

In the initial position (**Rioja**) or when doubled (**guitarra**), the **r** is strongly trilled.

The following words contain either a normally trilled **r** (as in **mira**) or a strongly trilled **r** (as in **terraza**). Can you tell the two different **r** sounds apart? Which words have a normally trilled **r**, and which have a strongly trilled **r**? Mark the two **r** sounds, each in a different way, and check your answers in the companion book. Finally, listen to the words again and repeat them.

mira — terraza — Rosita — guerrilla — claro — estantería — Rioja —
ahora — garaje — guitarra — lavadora — euro

Looking at the apartment

6

Read the following sentences and turns of phrase from the dialogue while listening to them on the CD. Pay attention to the intonation of the declarative statements and exclamations. Repeat the sentences several times. Then take a look at the translations.

1. ¡Qué linda!

2. Es muy bonita.

3. Es muy grande.

4. ¡Estupendo!

a. *How pretty!*

b. *She is very pretty.*

c. *It is very big.*

d. *Great!*

5. ¡Qué lujo!

6. ¿Necesitas algo más?

7. Estoy muy cansada.

e. *What luxury!*

f. *Do you need anything else?*

g. *I am very tired.*

8. ¿No quieres tomar nada?

9. Muchas gracias por todo.

10. ¡Hasta luego!

h. *Wouldn't you like something to drink?*

i. *Thanks very much for everything.*

j. *See you later!*

7

Listen to the dialogue. Read the following sentences and indicate whether they are true or false. If you're not sure, you can read the translation of the entire dialogue in the companion book.

	true	false
1. Rosita is enthusiastic about the kitchen.		
2. The apartment has only one bathroom.		
3. There's a terrace off Rosita's room.		
4. Chema's room is tidy.		
5. Chema offers Rosita something to drink.		
6. Rosita is tired and would like to rest.		

veintiuno | 21

Stress — Forming the plural of nouns and articles

8

poquito — ▶
a (little) bit
cenamos — *we eat dinner*
usted — *you* (pol.)
el catalán — *Catalan*
el número — *number*

▶ **§ 3 Stress and Written Accents**

Listen to the following words on the CD, and underline the stressed syllables.

     1. poquito   2. cenamos   3. usted   4. catalán   5. número

Words that end in a vowel (**-a, -e, -i, -o, -u**) or in **-n, -s** are stressed on the next to last syllable: **Poquito, cenamos**

Words that end in a consonant (other than **n** and **s**) are stressed on the last syllable: **Usted**

Words whose stress deviates from the preceding rules have a written accent marking the stressed syllable: **Catalán**

Words that are stressed on the second syllable from the last also have a written accent: **Número**

9

▶ **§ 5 Nouns**

The plural is formed by adding an **-s** to words that end in a vowel (**a, e, i, o, u**):

     cocina + s ▶ cocina**s**   dormitorio + s ▶ dormitorio**s**

For words that end in a consonant, add **-es**:

la ciudad —
city, town ▶

     mujer + es ▶ mujer**es**   ciudad + es ▶ ciudad**es**

Words that have a written accent on the last syllable in the singular lose it in the plural:

     salón + es ▶ salones

Form the plural of the following words:

     viaje — hotel — balcón — sombrero

10

▶ **§ 4 Articles**

Good to know:
In the plural, the indefinite article may be omitted: **Tengo buenos amigos en Madrid.** *— I have good friends in Madrid.*

Complete the following sentences by using the appropriate article. The plural forms of the articles are **los / las** and **unos / unas**.

     1. ¿Quieres ver _____ baños?

     2. ¿Tomamos _____ cervezas?

     3. _____ amigas de Rosita son de México.

     4. Tenemos _____ cuartos muy bonitos, ¿verdad?

Adjectives

11

Adjectives agree in number and gender with the noun they modify.
· Adjectives that end in **-o** require **-a** for the feminine form:
    el escritorio pequeño   **una cocina pequeña**
· All other adjectives generally have only one form for masculine and
  feminine:
    una cama grande / un piso grande
    una mujer normal / un hombre normal
Adjectives of nationality ending in a consonant are exceptions to this rule:
    español — española

For the plural, the same rules apply as for nouns. Listen to the following
three sentences containing plurals, and concentrate on the endings. Then
say the sentences out loud.

> **Good to know:**
> Adjectives usually,
> but not always, follow
> the noun they modify:
> **¡Buenos días!** (by
> the way: **el día** is
> masculine!).
> Adjectives always
> agree with the noun
> they modify: **La**
> **cocina es pequeña.**
> — *The kitchen is*
> *small.*

▶ § 6 Adjectives

TR. 22 🔵1

1. Los escritorios son nuevos.   2. Las camas son grandes.

           3. Los hombres son españoles.

Este / esta (this) can be used as adjectives (with a noun: **Este piso es boni-**
to) or as pronouns (without a noun: **Éste es Jordi**). **Esto** is considered neuter
and always stands alone, with no written accent: **Esto es el salón**.

12 ✏️

Look at the pictures and mark the adjective that goes with each. Make sure
the adjectives agree with the nouns. You will find the translations of new
words in the vocabulary box on the right.

dos armarios
☐ nuevas
☐ pequeños
☐ enorme

un sofá
☐ pequeña
☐ enormes
☐ nuevo

> ◀ **la mesa** — *table*
> **la silla** — *chair*
> **moderno / a** —
> *modern*
> **elegante** — *elegant*
> **enorme** —
> *enormous*

dos sillas
☐ bonitos
☐ elegante
☐ modernas

una mesa
☐ pequeñas
☐ bonita
☐ pequeño

*Regular verbs ending in **-ar***

13 TR. 23

Good to know:
Only the first person singular of **estar** is irregular (**estoy**). Please note the written accents in some forms:

estoy	estamos
estás	estáis
está	están

▶ §13 Regular Verbs

Read the following sentences and supply the missing verbs after listening to sentences 1 and 3 on the CD.

1. ¿ _____ algo más? — Ahora sólo _____ mi cama.

2. Chema cena en la cocina.

3. ¿Jordi y tú cenáis en el salón? — No, _____ en la cocina.

4. Rosita, Chema y Jordi necesitan dos baños.

Take another look at the verb forms above. All regular verbs ending in **-ar,** such as **necesitar** and **cenar**, are conjugated as follows:

necesit-<u>o</u>	necesit-<u>amos</u>
necesit-<u>as</u>	necesit-<u>áis</u>
necesit-<u>a</u>	necesit-<u>an</u>

The endings are attached to the verb stem (what's left after the ending **-ar** is removed: for example, **necesit-**).

14 TR. 24

Listen to the following sentences and place the verb forms in the correct blanks. Listen to the sentences again and repeat them. The translations of new words appear in the vocabulary box at left.

bailar — *to dance*
el momento — *moment*

Good to know:
In Spanish, modal verbs such as *can, must, shall* are not very frequently used. If you want to make a suggestion, you can say directly:
¿Cenamos en el restaurante?

toma — cenamos — necesito — estás — bailáis — están

1. ¿ _____ muy cansada del viaje?

2. _____ el baño un momento.

3. ¿ _____ en el restaurante?

4. Los dormitorios _____ desordenados.

5. ¿Vosotros _____ flamenco?

6. Chema _____ un café.

15 ✎

We can negate a sentence by using the word **no. No** always precedes the verb.

Do you remember the dialogues in Lessons 1 and 2? Look at the following sentences and indicate whether they are true (**correcto**) or false (**falso**). If you're not sure, you can read through the dialogue in the companion book again.

▶ § 24 Negations

	correcto	falso
I. Chema no es mexicano.		
2. La cocina del piso no es grande.		
3. El salón no es pequeño.		
4. El cuarto de Rosita no tiene balcón.		

Good to know:
In Spanish, the double negative does not make a statement positive; it remains a negation.

In the dialogue, Chema asks Rosita: **¿No quieres tomar nada?** Literally, that means *Wouldn't you like to drink nothing?* If the word **nada** follows the verb, Spanish requires a double negative of this kind.

16 [TR. 25] ✎

Draw a line connecting the questions on the left with the appropriate answers on the right. Then listen to the three responses on the CD and repeat them. The translation of new expressions appears in the vocabulary box on the right.

◀ **soy de … —**
I come from / I'm from …
hoy — *today*

I. Tú eres española, ¿no?	a. Sí. Hoy está un poco desordenado.
2. ¿Quieres tomar algo?	b. No, soy de México.
3. Éste es tu cuarto, ¿verdad?	c. No, gracias. Estoy muy cansada.

Good to know:
In the sentence **No, soy de México**, a comma must follow **No**, and if you are speaking you need to pause; otherwise, a negation will result. **No soy de México** means *I'm not from Mexico*.

17 [TR. 26]

You already know the numbers from 0 to 9. Listen to the numbers from 10 to 19 on the CD. Pay attention to the pronunciation, and repeat the numbers several times.

IO	diez	I4	catorce	I7	diecisiete
II	once	I5	quince	I8	dieciocho
I2	doce	I6	dieciséis	I9	diecinueve
I3	trece				

▶ § 38 Numbers

Languages in Spain — Intercultural tip: Madrid

18

Good to know:

Unlike Spain's other languages, Basque is not derived from Latin, but is a pre-Roman language. Its name in Basque is **euskera.**

Although Spanish is spoken in Latin America and in Spain, Spain has other official languages as well. Do you know what they are? Listen to the names of the languages on the CD and repeat them. Then write them in the correct boxes on the map.

gallego — vasco (euskera) — catalán — español

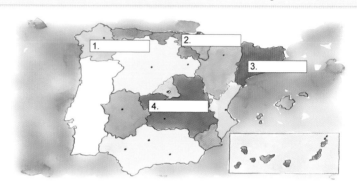

19

Madrid, the capital of Spain, has more than 3 million inhabitants. The city has a climate with hot summers and relatively cold winters.

Among the highlights of a visit are sure to be the **Puerta del Sol,** the true center of the city, the **Plaza Mayor**, one of Madrid's best-known and most impressive public squares, or the marvelous art museums, **El Prado** and the **Museo de Arte Moderno Reina Sofía**. Additional places to see are the **Parque del Retiro**, probably the most beautiful park in Madrid, where you can take wonderful walks or even go for a boat trip on a lake. For something completely different in Madrid, visit the gigantic flea market, known as **El Rastro.**

Madrid is an extremely lively city, with cafés, discos, and a nightlife that never stops. In summer, there's nothing nicer than having a drink out on one of the countless, beautiful summer terraces.

Getting acquainted — Saying good-bye

1 TR. 28

Here you'll get acquainted with the characters who appear in this lesson. Listen to the CD and hear how Rosita, Agustín, and Noelia introduce themselves to each other. Then look at the translations below and match them with the appropriate Spanish sentences.

3. Yo me llamo Agustín.

5. Trabajo en una empresa internacional.

1. Me llamo Rosita y soy de México.

4. Soy jefe del departamento de ventas.

2. Trabajo en un museo de Madrid.

6. Yo soy Noelia, la hija de Agustín.

7. Estudio en la universidad.

■ a. *I work for an international firm.* ■ b. *My name is Rosita, and I'm from Mexico.*
■ c. *I'm studying at the university.* ■ d. *I'm Noelia, Agustín's daughter.* ■ e. *I work at a museum in Madrid.* ■ f. *I'm the head of the sales department.* ■ g. *My name is Agustín.*

2 TR. 29

Now listen to the way people say good-bye in Spanish, and repeat the expressions.

¡Adiós, buenas noches!	*Good-bye, good evening / good night!*
¡Hasta pronto!	*See you soon!*
¡Hasta mañana!	*See you tomorrow!*
¡Hasta la próxima semana!	*See you next week!*
¡Hasta luego!	*See you later!*

Rosita meets her neighbors

3

It's already been two days since Rosita arrived in Madrid. She's just leaving the apartment, and she runs into her neighbor Agustín Giménez and his 19-year-old daughter, Noelia, who are just coming home.

Look at the pictures and listen to the dialogue on the CD several times. You'll notice that you understand it a little better each time.

4

Listen to the dialogue again and read the sentences below. Who says what? Write the numbers in the correct boxes below. If you're not sure, just listen to the dialogue again. Then read the translations below.

1.

2.

3.

- ▦ a. Tengo una beca de investigación.
- ▦ b. ¿De dónde eres?
- ▦ c. Estoy muy contenta.
- ▦ d. Administración de Empresas.
- ▦ e. Muchas gracias, muy amable.
- ▦ f. Usted es la nueva vecina, ¿verdad?
- ▦ g. ¡Me encanta México!
- ▦ h. Adiós, ¡igualmente!
- ▦ i. Me gusta mucho.
- ▦ j. Y usted, ¿cómo se llama?

Y usted, ¿cómo se llama? — *And you? What's your name?*
Tengo una beca de investigación. — *I have a research fellowship.*
Estoy muy contenta. — *I'm very happy.*
Muchas gracias, muy amable. — *Thank you, that's very kind.*
Usted es la nueva vecina, ¿verdad? — *You're the new neighbor, aren't you?*

¡Me encanta México! — *I love Mexico!*
Administración de Empresas — *Business Administration*
¿De dónde eres? — *Where are you from?*
Adiós, igualmente. — *Me too. Good-bye!*
Me gusta mucho. — *I like it very much.*

Getting acquainted

5

Listen to some of the sentences from the dialogue and repeat each one.
Then look at the translations.

1. Me llamo Rosita Yáñez.
2. ¡Bienvenida!
3. Muchas gracias, muy amable.
4. Es mi hija.
5. Por supuesto.
6. Me gusta mucho.
7. Soy mexicana, de la capital.
8. ¡Es un país fantástico!
9. Y tú, Noelia, ¿qué haces?
10. Encantado de conocerte.

a. *My name is Rosita Yáñez.*
b. *Welcome!*
c. *Thank you, that's very kind.*
d. *She is my daughter.*
e. *Of course.*
f. *I like it very much.*
g. *I'm a Mexican, from the capital.*
h. *It's a fabulous country!*
i. *And you, Noelia, what do you do?*
j. *Pleased to meet you.*

6

Listen to the dialogue again, and this time read along in the companion
book. It contains many words and expressions that you're familiar with
now, such as **¡Buenas tardes!** Underline the parts you already know. Then
look at the words and expressions that you haven't yet learned. Can you
guess their meaning? Just give it a try! Then you can check your guesses
against the translation of the dialogue in the companion book.

Don't get annoyed if you run into a passage full of new words. Try
to guess the meaning by looking for similarities with your native
language or another language you may know. The meaning of many
words can be guessed from the context. Don't get discouraged if you
don't understand every word right off the bat; instead, focus on all
that you've learned thus far.

Reflexive verbs — Indirect pronouns

7

▶ § 22 Reflexive Verbs

Reflexive verbs are verbs that are always accompanied by a reflexive pronoun (myself, yourself, himself, …). The verb **llamar<u>se</u>** (*to be named*, literally: *To call oneself*) is one such example.

Listen to the following sentences on the CD, and put the verb forms in the correct blanks.

> os llamáis — te llamas — me llamo — nos llamamos — se llama

1. Yo _____ Rosita. Y tú, ¿cómo _____?

2. ¿Cómo _____ ella?

3. Nosotros _____ Giménez. Y vosotros,

   ¿cómo _____?

Pay attention to the position of the pronoun: It immediately precedes the conjugated verb (but it is attached to the infinitive form: **llamarse**). Next, look at all the forms of the verb **llamarse**.

(yo) **me llamo**	(nosotros / nosotras) **nos llamamos**
(tú) **te llamas**	(vosotros / vosotras) **os llamáis**
(él / ella / usted) **se llama**	(ellos / ellas / ustedes) **se llaman**

Now answer this question: **Y usted, ¿cómo se llama?**

8

▶ § 27 Indirect
      Pronouns

Good to know:

Pay attention to the article: **Me gusta el café.** (*I like coffee.*)

Good to know:

le gusta can mean *she likes / he likes / you like* (polite singular form of address).

Noelia thinks Rosita's accent is pretty, so she says: **Me gusta mucho.** Agustín really is enthusiastic about Mexico: **¡Me encanta México!** You say **me gusta** when you like something or someone; you use **me encanta** when you're very enthusiastic about something, when you like it a great deal. These forms require an indirect pronoun.

> **¿Te gusta el piso, Rosita? — Sí, <u>me</u> gusta mucho.**
> *Do <u>you</u> like the apartment, Rosita? Yes, <u>I</u> like it very much.*

Now look at the other indirect pronouns.

1. ¿**Le** gusta la sangría?   a. *Does **she** / Does **he** / Do **you** like sangria?*
2. **Nos** encanta la paella.   b. *We are crazy about paella.*
3. ¿**Os** gusta Madrid?   c. *Do **you** like Madrid?*
4. ¿**Les** gusta bailar?   d. *Do **you** / **they** like to dance?*

Literally, the last sentence means *Is it pleasing **to you** to dance?* Here the *you* is plural; that is, several people are being addressed. The pronoun can also mean *they*, if the question is being asked about other people: *Is it pleasing **to them** to dance?*

*Regular verbs ending in **-er** — The verb **tener***

9

The expressions **me gusta** or **me encanta** refer to things or activities. When the thing you like is plural, the verb also has to be plural: **Me gustan / en-cantan los restaurantes españoles.** Fill in the blanks in the following sentences with forms of **gustar** or **encantar**.

1. Me _____ los museos.

2. ¿Os _____ la paella?

3. Me _____ mucho trabajar en el museo.

4. ¿Les _____ las habitaciones, señores?

◀ **la habitación** — *room*

10 TR. 33

From the last lesson, you already know some verbs ending in **-ar**, such as **cenar**. When Chema shows Rosita the living room, he says: **Y éste es el salón. Aquí comemos y cenamos.** The verb **comer** belongs to a different group, the group of verbs ending in **-er**.

Using the conjugation of **cenar** (see conjugation at right) as a model, try to guess the forms of **comer**. Write the endings in the table on the right, and then compare the results with the forms on the CD.

Some verbs are irregular only in the first person singular:

hacer *(to make, to do)*: **yo hago**   **conocer** *(to know, to meet)*: **yo conozco**

ver *(to see)*: **yo veo**   **saber** *(to know)*: **yo sé**

▶ **§ 13 Regular Verbs**

cenar

cen-o	cen-amos
cen-as	cen-áis
cen-a	cen-an

comer

com-___	com-___
com-___	com-___
com-___	com-___

11 TR. 34

Listen to and look at the following sentences, and mark the forms of the verb **tener** that are formed <u>differently</u> from those of **comer**.

1. Tengo una beca de investigación.
2. Tienes un acento precioso.
3. El piso tiene dos baños.
4. ¿Tenéis terraza en el piso? — No, pero tenemos balcón.
5. Los Giménez tienen en casa un horno microondas.

Good to know:
Please note: **Tengo 10 años.** — *I'm 10 years old.*

Now write all the forms of **tener** in the conjugation box on the right.

tener

_____	_____
_____	_____
_____	_____

*Verbs ending in -**ar** and -**er** — **ser** and **estar***

12

Complete the sentences with the correct verb forms.

1. ¿Cómo (*llamarse*) _____ ustedes?

2. Yo (*comer*) _____ en la cocina; Ana (*comer*) _____ en el salón.

3. ¿Vosotras (*trabajar*) _____ o (*estudiar*) _____ en la universidad?

4. Yo (*estar*) _____ muy cansado, ¿y tú?

5. Nosotros no (*tener*) _____ horno microondas en la cocina.

6. Rosita (*tener*) _____ una beca de investigación.

7. Tú (*llamarse*) _____ Noelia y (*ser*) _____ de Madrid, ¿verdad?

beber — *to drink* ▶

8. Nosotros no (*beber*) _____ cerveza. — Y vosotros, ¿(*beber*) _____ cerveza?

13

▶ § 19 ser / estar

Fill in the blanks with the appropriate forms of **ser** and **estar**, and check your answers by using the CD. What is the difference between **ser** and **estar**? By looking at the examples, try to come up with a rule. Compare it with the explanation below.

somos — estoy — está — es

1. _____ muy contenta en Madrid.

2. México _____ un país fantástico.

3. La habitación _____ desordenada.

el médico — *doctor,* ▶
physician

4. Nosotros _____ médicos.

The verb **ser** is used for giving the following information:

· Name (**Soy Chema.**)
· Nationality (**¿Eres mexicana?**)
· Occupation (**Soy jefe de ventas.**)
· Inherent states or conditions (**Noelia es muy inteligente.**)

In contrast, the verb **estar** expresses a temporary or accidental condition: **Estoy cansada.**

Adjectives of nationality — Occupations

14

Adjectives of nationality that end in **-o** require the ending **-a** for the feminine form: **mexicano — mexicana**
Adjectives of nationality that end in a consonant form the feminine by adding **-a**: **español — española**
Adjectives of nationality that end in **-e** remain unchanged: **estadounidense** *(American, from the U.S.)*
The formation of the plural follows the pattern of the nouns.

> ▶ **§ 7 Adjectives of Nationality**

 TR. 36

What is the nationality of these people? Listen to the adjectives of nationality on the CD, and fill in the blanks with the correct forms. Pay attention to gender and number.

1. Claudine y Isabelle son de París, Francia. Son _____ .

2. Hans y Anja son de Berna, Suiza. Son _____ .

3. Marisa y Cecilia son de Santiago, Chile. Son _____ .

4. Jane y Charles son de Londres, Inglaterra. Son _____ .

5. Ana es de Lisboa, Portugal. Es _____ .

6. Rita y Julia son de Ottawa, Canadá. Son _____ .

7. La señora Ylva es de Estocolmo, Suecia. Es _____ .

8. Jean y Claire son de Bruselas, Bélgica. Son _____ .

15 **TR. 37**

Look at the pictures and write the titles of occupations under the appropriate pictures. Then check your answers with the CD.

> **Good to know:**
> Some titles of occupations have both a masculine and a feminine form (**el médico — la médica**) *(doctor)*, while others use the same form for both genders: **el / la estudiante** *(student)*.

profesora — arquitecta — taxista — fotógrafo — secretaria — ingeniero

1.	2.	3.	4.	5.	6.

_____ _____ _____ _____ _____ _____

Role play: Getting acquainted — Intercultural tip: Mexico City

16

Two neighbors — Felipe Iriarte and Antonio Ramos — meet in the stairwell for the first time. Listen to the dialogue on the CD, paying close attention to what Antonio Ramos says.
Play the role of Antonio Ramos, and complete the dialogue with your own information.

> *Felipe Iriarte:* ¡Hola, buenos días!

You return his greeting: _____

> *Felipe Iriarte:* Yo soy el nuevo vecino. Me llamo Felipe Iriarte.

You introduce yourself as well: _____

> *Felipe Iriarte:*¿Es usted de Madrid?

You say where you're from: _____

> *Felipe Iriarte:* Ah, ¡qué interesante! ¿Y qué hace usted aquí?

You state your occupation and ask what he does:

_____

> *Felipe Iriarte:* Yo soy economista y trabajo en un banco. Bueno, pues,
>
> mucho gusto.

You say good-bye: _____

> *Felipe Iriarte:* Hasta pronto.

17

Mexico City (**México D.F.**) is a capital city of truly enormous dimensions. Between 20 and 28 million people, depending on the estimate, live and survive here — that is one fourth of the entire population of Mexico. The city, which is 7,350 feet above sea level, was founded by the Aztecs, who named it **Tenochtitlán**.
The **Zócalo** is the main square in the center of town; in its vicinity you will find the major places of interest, such as the cathedral (sixteenth century), the Aztec excavations, the shopping and entertainment district **Zona Rosa**, the boulevard **Paseo de la Reforma**, and the city park **Bosque de Chapultepec**. Farther south is the university with its renowned library.
About 19 miles north of the capital is the spectacular Aztec city of pyramids, **Teotihuacán**.

Nouns of relationship — Personal belongings

1

Here you see the entire Giménez family. Listen to each family member introduce himself or herself on the CD, and repeat the sentences.

Good to know:
For **madre** and **padre**, you can also use **mamá** and **papá** — with an accent!
In Latin America, **esposo / esposa** is also used for *husband / wife*.

¡Hola! Yo soy la hermana de Nacho. Agustín y Charo son mis padres.

¡Hola! Yo soy el marido de Charo y el padre de Noelia y Nacho.

¡Buenas tardes! Yo soy la mujer de Agustín y la madre de Noelia y Nacho.

¡Hola! Yo soy el hijo de Agustín y Charo. Vivo en Inglaterra.

¡Buenas tardes! Yo soy la madre de Agustín y la abuela de Nacho y Noelia.

la abuela — *grandmother*	**el padre** — *father*
la hermana — *sister*	**los padres** — *parents*
el hijo — *son*	**vivo (vivir)** — *I live (to live)*
la madre — *mother*	**Inglaterra** — *England*

2

Read these words and decide which article goes with each. Write the articles in the blanks, and use the CD to check your answers.

____ agenda   ____ móvil   ____ monedero   ____ llaves   ____ gafas   ____ bolígrafo

Charo looks for her purse

3

There's a lot of excitement in the apartment of the Giménez family, the neighbors of Rosita, Chema, and Jordi. Charo Giménez, the mother, is desperately searching for her purse.

Listen to the dialogue on the CD. The pictures will help you understand what's going on.

4 TR. 42

On the CD, listen to the following expressions taken from the dialogue and read them at the same time. Listen to the sentences again and repeat them. Then look at the translations.

1. ¿Dónde está mi bolso?

2. Aquí está.

3. ¡Ya lo tengo!

a. *Where is my purse?*

b. *Here it is.*

c. *I have it!*

4. No lo veo.

5. ¿Sabes dónde está?

6. Quizá lo sabe la abuela

d. *I don't see it.*

e. *Do you know where it is?*

f. *Maybe Grandmother know.*

7. ¡Falta dinero!

8. ¡En esta casa hay un ladrón!

9. ¡Tranquila, mamá!

g. *Some money is missing!*

h. *There's a thief in this house!*

i. *Calm down, Mom!*

Talking about personal belongings

5

Paying close attention, listen to the entire dialogue on the CD once more. Read the questions pertaining to the dialogue and mark the correct answers. There is only one correct answer in each case! For the translations of new words, see the vocabulary box on the right.

1. ¿Dónde está el bolso de Charo?
   a. ■ en el salón
   b. ■ en el cuarto
   c. ■ en la cocina

2. ¿Qué hay en el bolso?
   a. ■ un móvil
   b. ■ un monedero
   c. ■ un bolígrafo

¿cuánto? — *how much?*
el dinero — *money*
falta (faltar) — *is missing*
hay — *there is, there are*
el parque — *park*

3. En el piso viven …
   a. ■ Charo y Noelia.
   b. ■ Noelia y los padres.
   c. ■ los padres, la hija y la abuela.

4. ¿Dónde está la abuela?
   a. ■ en su cuarto
   b. ■ en el parque
   c. ■ en la cocina

5. ¿Cuánto dinero falta?
   a. ■ más de 40 (cuarenta) euros
   b. ■ 14 (catorce) euros
   c. ■ 4 (cuatro) euros

6

Listen to the dialogue on the CD once more, while reading the text in the companion book.
Can you tell from the dialogue how to say "I don't know [it]" in Spanish? Write the sentence in the balloon below.

If you like, you can now look at the translation of the entire dialogue in the companion book.

Regular verbs ending in -ir — Demonstratives

7

▶ §13 Regular Verbs

You're already familiar with infinitives ending in **-ar** and **-er**. Spanish has a third conjugation as well, verbs ending in **-ir**, such as **vivir**. The conjugational endings of **-er** and **-ir** verbs are identical, with the exception of the forms for **nosotros / -as** and **vosotros / -as**. The forms of **vivir** that are missing in the exercise here are identical to the forms of **-er** verbs (such as **comer**). Listen to the sentences on the CD and fill in the missing forms.

TR. 43

1. Yo _____ en Barcelona y tú, ¿dónde _____?

2. La familia Giménez _____ en Madrid.

3. Vosotros vivís en Argentina, ¿verdad? — Sí, vivimos en la capital.

4. Rosita, Chema y Jordi _____ en el mismo piso.

Finally, write all the endings for **vivir** in the conjugation box on the left.

vivir	
viv-_____	viv-_____
viv-_____	viv-_____
viv-_____	viv-_____

8
TR. 44

Write down all the forms of the verbs **trabajar, comer,** and **vivir**. If you need help, you can hear all the verb forms on the CD.

9

▶ §33 Demonstratives

The forms **este / esta / estos / estas** (*this / these*) refer to certain objects or persons that are in the immediate vicinity of the speaker. They can be used alone or in connection with a noun, with which they agree in gender and number.
Look at the following sentences, choose the correct form for each, and write it in the blank.

el árbol — *tree*　▶

1. En _____ casa hay un ladrón. (*este/estas/esta*)

2. _____ balcones son muy grandes. (*esta/estos/estas*)

3. En _____ parque hay muchos árboles. (*este/estos/esta*)

4. _____ llaves son de Chema, ¿no? (*estos/estas/esta*)

The form **esto** refers to something that is not specified, and it always is used alone: **¿Qué es <u>esto</u>? — Es un bolso.**

estar and *hay* — Possessives

10

Hay is the impersonal form of **haber** (*to have*) and it never changes. **Hay** means *there is*, *there are* and does not refer to a definite thing or person. Therefore, the indefinite article follows **hay**: **¡En esta casa hay un ladrón!** **Estar**, on the other hand, refers to definite things or persons. Therefore, **estar** is followed by the noun with its definite article: **¿Dónde está la abuela?**

As you may recall, Noelia has a brother, Nacho, who lives in England. Here he gives some information about himself, but the correct forms of **ser, estar,** and **hay** are missing. Fill in the blanks.

> ¡Hola! Me llamo Nacho y _____ el hijo de Agustín y Charo.
>
> Ahora _____ en Londres, donde estudio inglés. _____
>
> una ciudad fascinante. _____ muchos museos, tiendas y …
>
> "pubs". Vivo en un piso compartido con dos chicos, Carlos y
>
> Mauricio. _____ venezolanos y muy simpáticos. Uno
>
> _____ estudiante de Medicina y el otro trabaja
>
> de camarero. La verdad es que _____ muy
>
> contento aquí.

▶ § 20 **hay / está** or **están**

◀ **fascinante** — *fascinating*
la tienda — *store, shop*
simpático/a — *pleasant, congenial*
la medicina — *medicine*

11

Here you see the Spanish possessives:

<u>mi</u> bolso y <u>mi</u> agenda	<u>nuestro</u> bolso y <u>nuestra</u> agenda
<u>tu</u> abuelo y <u>tu</u> abuela	<u>vuestro</u> abuelo y <u>vuestra</u> abuela
<u>su</u> hijo y <u>su</u> hija	<u>su</u> hijo y <u>su</u> hija

Only the forms **nuestro / a** and **vuestro / a** agree in gender with the object they refer to. To form the plural, add an **-s**: **Mis bolsos / nuestras abuelas.**

▶ § 34 Possessives

Good to know:

The form **su** can mean *his, her, its, their, your, one's.*

> Fill in the blanks with the correct possessives.
>
> 1. (*his*) _____ abuelo es cubano.
>
> 2. ¿Cómo se llama (*your* fam. pl.) _____ hija?
>
> 3. Señores, ¿dónde está (*your* pol. pl.) _____ jefe?
>
> 4. (*our*) _____ piso es muy grande.

Direct and indirect object pronouns

12

§ 26   Direct Object Pronouns

When Charo is looking for her coin purse in the dialogue, she says: **¿Y mi monedero? No lo veo. Lo** is a direct object pronoun. It refers to something that has just been mentioned (here **lo** refers to **el monedero**). **Lo** can also stand for an entire sentence:
¿Sabes dónde está mi monedero? — No, no lo sé, mamá.

Now learn the other direct object pronouns. Listen to the following sentences and fill in the blanks with the correct direct object pronouns.

TR. 45

las — la — los

1. ¿Dónde está la abuela? No _____ veo.

2. No veo las gafas. ¿ _____ tienes tú?

3. Yo no tengo los 40 euros. _____ tiene la abuela.

By examining the sentences, you can draw these conclusions:
· The direct object pronouns agree in gender and number with the previously mentioned direct object.
· The direct object pronouns always immediately precede the verb.

13

In the sentences below, direct or indirect object pronouns are missing. Fill in the blanks with the appropriate pronouns.

nos — te — lo — les — se — las — os — me

la cosa — *thing*
sino — *but; except*
perdón — *pardon, forgiveness*

1. Yo soy Chema. Y tú, ¿cómo _____ llamas?

2. ¿Tienes tú las cosas? Yo no _____ tengo.

3. ¿ _____ gustan estas habitaciones, señores?

4. No _____ llamo María, sino Marisa.

5. A nosotros _____ encanta bailar.

6. ¿ _____ gusta nuestro piso?

7. ¿Dónde está el bolso? No _____ veo.

8. Perdón, señora, ¿cómo _____ llama usted?

The verb **saber** — *Other nouns of relationship*

14

On the CD, listen to some sentences containing forms of **saber** (*to know*).
Find these forms in the strings of letters below, and mark them.

1. denesabesanmiro
2. nedórbseroséleita
3. berosazsabemadase
4. sesabemosrsabéises
5. serossabenenanzaom

Now you can read the transcriptions of the sentences in the companion
book in order to check your answers. The first person singular is the only
irregular form of the verb **saber.** Finally, write all the forms of **saber** in the
conjugation box on the right.

saber
____   ____
____   ____
____   ____

15

On the CD, listen to Rosita as she introduces her family, and read along.
Some of the nouns of relationship are already familiar to you. Can you
guess the others with the help of the family tree below? Match the underlined words with the correct English equivalents.

1. Mis padres tienen tres hijos y tres <u>nietos</u>.
2. Lourdes es la <u>madre</u> de Luis Miguel.
3. Marta es la <u>esposa</u> de Francisco y madre de Elena y Silvia.
4. Yo soy la <u>tía</u> de Luis Miguel, Elena y Silvia.
5. César es el <u>tío</u> de Elena y Silvia.
6. Francisco es mi <u>cuñado</u>.
7. Elena y Silvia son mis <u>sobrinas</u>.
8. Luis Miguel es mi <u>sobrino</u>.
9. César es mi <u>hermano</u>.
10. Luis es el <u>primo</u> de Elena y Silvia.

▨ nieces — ▨ mother — ▨ uncle — ▨ grandson — ▨ brother-in-law —
▨ cousin — ▨ wife — ▨ aunt — ▨ nephew — ▨ brother

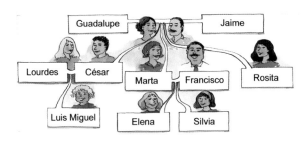

Numbers from 20 to 50 — Game: Bingo — Intercultural tip: Spanish names

16

▶ § 38 Numbers

Good to know:
Starting with 30, the tens and the ones are written as separate words: **treinta y uno.**

Now learn the numbers from 20 to 50. Listen to the numbers on the CD and repeat them.

20	veinte	23	veintitrés	45	cuarenta y cinco
21	veintiuno	31	treinta y uno	50	cincuenta
22	veintidós	34	treinta y cuatro		

17 TR. 49

Would you like to play bingo? The CD will call out the numbers for you. As soon as you hear a number that's on your bingo card, mark it. When you have four numbers in a row (horizontally, vertically, or diagonally), you have **¡Bingo!** But no cheating! Check the transcription in the companion book to make sure you really heard the right numbers.

25	5	13	48
38	9	30	42
11	36	44	20
41	18	6	10

30	8	35	42
41	2	1	39
22	4	25	32
36	10	47	38

17	49	24	2
4	12	28	33
1	20	5	36
7	21	13	14

18

In Spanish, people always have two last names: for example, **Eduardo López García.** The first surname here (**López**) normally is the father's first surname, and the second (**García**) is the mother's first surname. Often, however, only the first surname is used, as is the case with our character in this lesson, Agustín Giménez.

Double first names are also quite typical, for example, in the case of traditional names containing **María** or **José.** That explains why short forms of first names are very common in colloquial Spanish:

María Teresa ▶ Maite, José María ▶ Chema

The same thing happens with single first names, too:

Women's names: **Dolores ▶ Lola, Josefa ▶ Pepa, Mercedes ▶ Merche, Rosario ▶ Charo**

Men's names: **Francisco ▶ Paco, Ignacio ▶ Nacho, Javier ▶ Javi, Rafael ▶ Rafa**

Intercultural Tip

Questions and answers

1

What would you say in the following situations? Match the Spanish sentences with the appropriate situations. Then listen to the sentences on the CD and repeat them.

1. Creo que es muy inteligente.
2. ¿Qué significa "empresa"?
3. Me gusta mucho bailar.
4. Mucho gusto.
5. No lo sé.
6. ¡Adiós, buenas noches!
7. ¡De nada!
8. Quizás está en el bolso.

a. *Someone is being introduced to you.*
b. *You express ignorance of something.*
c. *You respond to someone's saying Thank you.*
d. *You express your opinion.*
e. *You ask what a word means.*
f. *You say what you enjoy doing.*
g. *You hazard a guess.*
h. *You say good-bye late in the evening.*

2

Read the questions and the answers for each, and then mark the answer that does <u>not</u> fit.

1. ¿Qué tal el viaje?
a. ▧ Un poco largo.
b. ▧ Fantástico.
c. ▧ Sí, es verdad.

2. ¿Estás cansada?
a. ▧ Estoy en mi cuarto.
b. ▧ Sí, mucho.
c. ▧ Sí, necesito una siesta.

3. ¿Tu piso tiene terraza?
a. ▧ No, pero balcón sí.
b. ▧ En el baño y en el pasillo.
c. ▧ Sí, pero es muy pequeña.

4. ¿Qué hace tu padre?
a. ▧ Trabaja en una oficina.
b. ▧ Es profesor.
c. ▧ Mi madre no trabaja.

5. ¿Tienes hijos?
a. ▧ Mi madre sí.
b. ▧ No, no tengo hijos.
c. ▧ Sí, un hijo, se llama Óscar.

6. ¿Sabes dónde están los chicos?
a. ▧ Creo que en el parque.
b. ▧ No lo sé.
c. ▧ Son muy simpáticos.

3

Listen to the question on the CD and mark the correct answer.

1. ▧ No, no lo sé.   2. ▧ No, no lo sabemos.   3. ▧ No, no lo sabe.

Responding correctly

4

Match the sentences on the left with the appropriate sentences on the right.

1. Encantado de conocerte.
2. Oye, somos vecinos …
   nos podemos tratar de tú, ¿no?
3. ¿No quieres tomar nada?
4. Si necesitas algo,
   ya sabes dónde vivimos.

a. No, gracias.
b. Igualmente, y ¡adiós!
c. Gracias, muy amable.
d. ¡Por supuesto!

5

On the CD, listen to four questions. Then match the answers with the appropriate questions. You are free to listen to the questions several times.

Question 1
Question 2
Question 3
Question 4

a. En Roma.
b. Soy de la capital.
c. Es fotógrafo.
d. Juanjo, ¿y tú?

6

Read the following questions or statements and chose the correct response to each.

1. ¿Os gusta mi casa?
a. ■ Está cansada.
b. ■ Es la cocina.
c. ■ ¡Es preciosa!

2. ¡Muchas gracias!
a. ■ ¡Por supuesto!
b. ■ ¡De nada!
c. ■ ¡Encantada!

7

Read the questions and give your own answers.

		sí	no
1.	¿Habla usted inglés?		
2.	¿Es ingeniero/a?		
3.	¿Trabaja en una empresa?		
4.	¿Vive en una ciudad?		
5.	¿Tiene hermanos?		
6.	¿Le gusta el flamenco?		
7.	¿Conoce Madrid?		
8.	¿Sabe dónde está Salamanca?		

*Articles, nouns, adjectives — **ser** and **estar***

8

Do you still remember the plural forms of the articles, as well as how to form the plural of nouns and adjectives? If not, you can refresh your knowledge in the Grammar section.

▶ § 4 Articles

▶ § 5 Nouns

▶ § 6 Adjectives

Look at the following sentences, and make them plural.

1. La amiga de Ana es una chica muy simpática.
2. El amigo de Antonio es un chico muy inteligente.

9

Complete the sentences with the adjectives given in parentheses.

1. El piso tiene unas habitaciones muy (*large*) _____ .

2. Estos sofás son (*pretty*) _____ , ¿verdad?

3. México es un país muy (*interesting*) _____ .

10

Do you remember the difference between **ser** and **estar**?
Ser is used to state your name, identity, origin, nationality, and inherent or lasting characteristics of persons and things (description).
Estar is used to show location or position and to express a state or condition that is accidental or temporary.
Now fill in the blanks with the appropriate verbs.

▶ § 19 ser / estar

> estamos — somos — soy — están — eres — son — es — está

1. Yo trabajo en Madrid. _____ arquitecta.

2. El móvil _____ encima del sofá.

3. Ésta _____ mi hermana Carmen.

4. Chema y yo _____ muy contentos con nuestro trabajo.

5. ¡Qué simpáticos _____ tus amigos!

6. Nosotros _____ de Sevilla, ¿y vosotros?

7. ¿Dónde _____ tus padres?

8. ¿De dónde _____ , Ana?

ser, estar, hay — *Verbs in the present tense*

11

▶ § 20 **hay / está** or **están**

Fill in the blanks with the appropriate verbs.

1. La agenda _____ en mi oficina.

2. En este parque _____ árboles enormes.

3. ¿ _____ tus primas en casa?

4. En el salón _____ tres sillones muy bonitos.

hay
está
hay
están

The forms **está / están** are used to refer to a definite person or thing. They occur, for example, with the definite article.
The form **hay** is used when no definite thing or person is meant. **Hay** is used with the indefinite article, with words in the plural that are not accompanied by an article, or with numbers.

12

ser, estar, or **hay?** Choose the correct verb for each sentence.

1. La oficina _____ muy desordenada. (*hay/está/es*)

2. En el piso _____ dos baños. (*están/son/hay*)

3. El sofá _____ pequeño, pero bonito. (*es/hay/está*)

13

▶ § 13 Regular Verbs

▶ § 14 Irregular Verbs

Complete the following sentences with the verbs given in parentheses, and write the correct forms in the blanks. If you need help with the verb forms, check the Grammar section.

1. Mis abuelos (*vivir*) _____ en la capital.

2. Oye, y tú, ¿cómo (*llamarse*) _____?

3. Mira, éstos (*ser*) _____ mis amigos.

4. ¿Vosotros (*saber*) _____ de dónde es ella?

5. Yo (*tener*) _____ treinta y dos años, ¿y tú?

6. Nosotros siempre (*comer*) _____ en la cocina.

7. Mi padre (*trabajar*) _____ en un banco.

8. ¡Me (*encantar*) _____ los viajes!

Personal belongings — Furniture — Occupations

14 ✎

Write the 12 words given below in the appropriate columns of the table.
There should be a total of four words in each category.

En el piso	En la empresa	En el bolso

llaves — dormitorio — ingeniero — agenda — departamento —
sillón — armario — jefe — pasillo — gafas — secretaria — móvil

15 ✎

In the grid below, find the words that go with these pictures (horizontally/
vertically/ diagonally). Have fun hunting for them!

1.

2.

3.

```
C V N E R Z O T P L E
O E B P O S F P S S S
R A N Q L J D E O Y C
D O C O R D J R F D R
E Q B E C S I C Á E I
N X E S R A U S H R T
A A R A T O M V G T O
D U O L U C Z A F V R
O Z S M E S A E O C I
R R E R S L S R L Q O
F B O L Í G R A F O X
```

4.

5.

6.

7.

Nouns of relationship

16

On the CD, listen to what Chema says about the members of the Giménez family, and read along. Do you know who he's talking about? Write the names in the blanks that follow the descriptions.

1. Es la madre de Agustín y la abuela de Nacho y Noelia. Le gusta mucho estar con sus amigas: _____

2. Es el marido de Charo y padre de Noelia y Nacho. Le encanta su trabajo: _____

3. Es el nieto de Doña Amparo. Le gusta estudiar inglés. Vive en Londres: _____

4. Es la mujer de Agustín y es la madre de Noelia y Nacho: _____

5. Es la hija de Agustín y Charo. Estudia en la universidad y es muy inteligente: _____

17

Look at the pictures and read the sentences next to them. How are these people related to Rosita? Mark the correct answers.

1. El hijo del hermano de Rosita es su
   a. ▪ primo.
   b. ▪ tío.
   c. ▪ sobrino.

2. El marido de la hermana de Rosita es su
   a. ▪ nieto.
   b. ▪ cuñado.
   c. ▪ padre.

3. La abuela de los sobrinos de Rosita es su
   a. ▪ madre.
   b. ▪ tía.
   c. ▪ hija.

Occupations — Numbers — A postcard from Mexico

18

What jobs are available? Put the letters in the right order to reveal the names of occupations.

1. paroresfo   2. atqetrocui   3. midacé

_____   _____   _____

19

The voice on the CD will dictate nine numbers to you. Write them down. Then listen to the numbers on the CD again and check what you have written.

20

Use the English words given below for help in filling in the blanks in the postcard Rosita got from her sister.

> *lives — you — are — apartment — how — sister — isn't it? — has*

¡Hola, Rosita!

¿_____ estás? Nosotros _____ bien. ¿Qué tal en Madrid?

¿_____ gusta la ciudad? ¿Tienes mucho trabajo en el museo?

¿Qué tal con Chema y Jordi? Y el _____ ... ¿es bonito? ¿Tiene

terraza? Mi amiga Lola también _____ ahora en Madrid; _____

una beca de investigación y trabaja en la universidad. Interesante,

¿_____ ?

La próxima semana te llamo por teléfono.

Besos. Tu _____ , Marta

The pronunciation of certain sounds — Listening to a dialogue

21 TR. 55

▶ § 2 Pronunciation

Read the eight comments on Spanish pronunciation. Which of the words given here contains the sound being described? Write the words in the appropriate blanks. Then use the CD to check your answers, and repeat the words aloud.

Chile — hola — Mallorca — queso — Gibraltar — cerveza — España — vela

1. The sound in this word resembles the **gn** in "cognac": _____

2. In initial position, **v** is pronounced like the **b** in "ballet": _____

3. The sound in this word is like the **ch** in "chocolate": _____

4. **c** before **e** and **i**, as well as **z**, are pronounced like the **th** in "thin":

_____

5. The sound in this word is like the **y** in "yes" or the **lli** in "million":

_____

6. The combination **qu** sounds like **k**: _____

7. **g** before **e** and **i**, as well as **j**, are pronounced like the **h** in "house":

_____

8. One letter in this word is silent: _____

22 TR. 56

Two coworkers — Elena and Diego — are getting acquainted. Listen to the dialogue between Elena and Diego on the CD. Then read the sentences below. Only one in each group applies to the dialogue. Listen to the dialogue again, and mark the correct sentences. If you like, you can look at the transcription of the dialogue in the companion book.

la administrativa ▶
— *office assistant*
la exportación
— *export*

1. a. ■ Elena es administrativa.
   b. ■ Elena es jefa de exportación.
   c. ■ Elena es secretaria.

2. a. ■ Ella es de Valencia.
   b. ■ Ella es de Barcelona.
   c. ■ Ella es de Valladolid.

3. a. ■ Le gusta mucho su ciudad.
   b. ■ Le gusta mucho tomar café.
   c. ■ Le gusta mucho su trabajo.

Leisure activities — Personal characteristics

1

What do the Giménez family and the three apartment mates do in their free time (**tiempo libre**)? Look at the pictures and listen to the four statements on the CD. Then match the leisure activities with the appropriate pictures.

I

2

3

4

a. por la noche tomar algo en un bar — b. por la tarde dar un paseo por el parque — c. ir al cine — d. el fin de semana ir a bailar

Por la noche tomar algo en un bar. — *To have a drink in a bar at night.* **El fin de semana ir a bailar.** — *To go dancing on the weekend.*

Por la tarde dar un paseo por el parque. — *To take a walk in the park in the afternoon.* **Ir al cine.** — *To go to the movies.*

2

Now you'll learn a little about what our characters are like. Listen to the following sentences on the CD and read along. Then underline the personal characteristics of the individual characters.

1. Noelia es una estudiante muy inteligente.
2. Rosita es una chica muy simpática.
3. Doña Amparo, abuela de Noelia, es una señora muy activa.
4. Agustín es siempre muy amable con sus vecinos.
5. Charo es una mujer un poquito nerviosa.
6. Chema es un chico un poco tímido pero es una persona muy interesante.

◀ **una señora activa** — *an active lady* **tímido/a** — *shy, timid*

Late in the evening at the Giménez apartment

3

Doña Amparo, the grandmother in the Giménez household, comes home late and Noelia, her granddaughter, arrives even later. Charo is still awake and talks to them about what they've been doing.
Look at the pictures and listen to the dialogue on the CD.

4

Who said what? Listen to the dialogue again. Then match the sentences with the speakers. You may already be able to guess the meaning of the sentences; compare your guesses with the translations below.

Good to know:

When **ir** (*to go*) and **irse** (*to go, to go away*) are used with information about destination, the difference has to do with the immediacy of the action:

Voy al museo means that I intend to go to the museum.

Me voy al museo means that I'm virtually on my way there.

1.

2.

3.

- ☐ a. No la he visto.
- ☐ b. Lo siento.
- ☐ c. ¡Hemos pasado la tarde allí!
- ☐ d. ¡Qué tarde llegas!
- ☐ e. ¡Me ha encantado!
- ☐ f. ¿De verdad?
- ☐ g. ¡Tengo mucho sueño!
- ☐ h. ¿Dónde ha estado?
- ☐ i. Me voy a la cama.

No la he visto. — *I haven't seen her.*
Lo siento. — *I'm sorry.*
¡Hemos pasado la tarde allí! — *We spent the evening there!*
¡Qué tarde llegas! — *You're really late coming home!*
¡Me ha encantado! — *I liked him a lot!*

¿De verdad? — *Really?*
¡Tengo mucho sueño! — *I'm very sleepy.*
¿Dónde ha estado? — *Where have you been?*
Me voy a la cama. — *I'm on my way to bed.*

Talking about leisure activities

5

Listen to the dialogue once more and mark the following statements as true or false. Before you answer, it's all right to listen to the dialogue several times. If you like, you can read the text simultaneously in the companion book.

	true	false
1. Grandmother has been out with her friends.		
2. Doña Amparo was at the movies.		
3. Charo asks her grandmother what bar they were in.		
4. The name of the film is *Pedro Almodóvar*.		
5. Doña Amparo wants to go to bed.		
6. Chema was in a bar with Paco.		
7. Noelia thinks that Chema is a boring person.		
8. Doña Amparo and Noelia met at Paco's bar.		

6

Now listen to the following sentences taken from the second part of the dialogue, and repeat them. Then you can read the translation of the entire dialogue in the companion book.

Charo: ¡Hola hija! ¡Qué tarde llegas!
Noelia: Es que he estado con Chema en el bar de Paco.
      ¡Hemos pasado la tarde allí!
Charo: ¿Quién es Chema?
Noelia: El vecino.
      Nos hemos encontrado en la calle
      y me ha invitado a tomar algo.
      Es un chico un poco tímido, pero muy amable y muy
      interesante.
Charo: ¿Y no has visto a la abuela en el bar de Paco?
Noelia: No, no la he visto.

Muy and mucho

7

▶ § 12 muy / mucho

Look at the following sentences from the dialogue for this lesson.

> ¡Es <u>muy</u> tarde!
> Nos hemos divertido <u>mucho</u>.
> ¿Le ha gustado, abuela? — ¡<u>Mucho</u>!
> Es un chico un poco tímido, pero <u>muy</u> amable y <u>muy</u> interesante.

When do you use **mucho**, and when do you use **muy**? Try to find some pattern, and complete the following exercise by filling in the blanks with **muy** or **mucho**.

1. Hola, ¿qué tal? — _____ bien, gracias.

2. Somos un piso _____ interesante.

3. Tienes un acento precioso. Me gusta _____ .

4. Noelia estudia _____ .

Have you managed to detect a pattern? Check your answers by applying the following rule:

mucho *(much; very; very much)* is used with verbs, as in these examples: **Me gusta mucho**; **comer mucho**.

muy *(very)* usually modifies an adjective or an adverb:
· With adjectives: **Muy amable**, **muy inteligente**
· With adjectives: **Muy tarde**, **muy bien**

8

Charo is very fond of her family and would like to tell you something about them. Fill in the blanks with **muy** or **mucho**. You will find the new words in the vocabulary box on the left.

la profesión — *occupation, profession*
pasear — *to take a walk*

Agustín, mi marido, tiene una profesión _____ interesante.

Trabaja _____ .

Mi hija Noelia estudia _____ . Es una chica _____ inteligente.

Mi hijo Nacho vive en Londres y está _____ contento.

El Retiro es un parque _____ grande y _____ bonito de

Madrid. A la abuela le gusta _____ ir a pasear allí con sus amigas.

The present perfect

9

The past tense form known as the **Pretérito Perfecto** (*present perfect*) consists of two elements: the present tense of the auxiliary verb **haber** (*to have*) and the past participle of a verb:

▶ **§ 15 Present Perfect**

- **¿Habéis visto esta película?** *(Have you seen this film?)*
- **Sí, ya la hemos visto.** *(Yes, we've already seen it.)*

The two elements of the present perfect must never be separated. Pronouns immediately precede the present perfect. The negation precedes the pronouns.

¿Y no has visto a la abuela en el bar de Paco? — No, no la he visto.

Good to know:
Unlike other languages such as German and French, which use different auxiliaries for transitive and intransitive verbs, Spanish always forms the perfect tenses with the verb **haber**.

TR. 61

Listen to the following sentences on the CD and write the missing forms of **haber** in the blanks.

1. _____ estado toda la tarde con mis amigas.

2. ¿Y no _____ visto a la abuela en el bar de Paco?

3. Pues ella también _____ estado allí.

4. ¿Y qué _____ hecho?

Now write all the forms of **haber** in the conjugation box on the right.

haber	
___	___
___	___
___	___

For verbs ending in **-ar**, the past participle is formed by adding **-ado** to the stem, while verbs ending in **-er** and **-ir** add **-ido** to the stem:

estar ▸ estado   **comer ▸ comido**   **vivir ▸ vivido**

Some verbs have irregular past participles:

ver ▸ visto   **hacer ▸ hecho**   **decir ▸ dicho**

10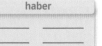

Fill in the blanks with the present perfect forms of the verbs provided.

1. Agustín y yo (*invitar*) _____ a nuestros amigos.

2. ¿ (*ver*) _____ tú la última película de Almodóvar?

3. Y vosotras, ¿ (*ir*) _____ de compras esta mañana?

◀ **ir de compras** — *to go shopping*

4. Yo nunca (*comer*) _____ paella, ¿y tú?

5. ¿Qué (*hacer*) _____ tus primos hoy?

6. El viaje a México (*ser*) _____ fantástico.

Use of the present perfect

11 👓

▶ § 15 Present Perfect

The present perfect is used in Spanish to discuss past events that, from the speaker's point of view, have a close connection with the present. Frequently the present perfect is used with expressions of time such as **este año** (*this year*), **este mes** (*this month*), **esta semana** (*this week*), and **hoy** (*today*):

- ¿Has ido al cine <u>esta semana</u>?
- Sí, he ido <u>hoy</u> y he visto una película muy buena.

12 🎧 TR. 62 ✏️

el **centro** — *center* ▶
nadar —*to swim*
la **piscina** —
swimming pool
el **deporte** — *sport*
los **Pirineos** —
Pyrenees
esquiar — *to ski*
un **par de veces** —
a couple of times
algún libro —
some/any book
recientemente
— *recently*
he **leído** (▶ **leer**)
— *to read*) — *I have read*
la **última novela** —
the latest novel

Our friends are really energetic! Listen to the five dialogues on the CD to learn what each of them has been doing. The pictures will help you understand the new expressions. Then match the sentences with the appropriate pictures.

I

2

3

4

5

a. Esta semana he hecho mucho deporte.

b. Este mes he leído la última novela de Isabel Allende.

c. Este año he esquiado un par de veces.

d. Hoy hemos ido de compras al centro.

e. Esta mañana hemos ido a nadar a la piscina.

Indicating the sequence of past events — Direct object pronouns

13

By using the following words, you can indicate the order in which past events occurred: **Primero** (*first*), **después** or **luego** (*then*), and **finalmente** (*finally*).

Rosita tells us what she did today. Read the sentences through, and underline the words Rosita uses to divide her story into time segments. Then listen to the sentences on the CD and repeat them.

> Primero he estado en el museo. Después he comido con unos colegas en un restaurante y luego hemos ido a pasear al parque del Retiro.

14 👓

The direct object pronouns for the third person — **lo, la, los, las** — are already familiar to you. There are other forms as well. Noelia says, for example: **Chema me ha invitado a tomar algo**. Here **me** is the direct object pronoun *me*. Here is a list of all the direct object pronouns:

▶ § 26 Direct Object
Pronouns

me *(me)*   **nos** *(us)*
te *(you)*   **os** *(you)*
lo / la *(him, it, you / her, it, you)*   **los / las** *(them, you)*

The direct object pronouns always immediately precede the verb.

15 🅣🅡.🅺🅸 ✏

Here you see four short dialogues. Which direct object pronouns are missing? Fill in the blanks with the correct pronouns, and use the CD to check your answers.

1. • ¿Has visto a Chema?

   ○ No, no _____ he visto. Creo que no ha llegado todavía.   me

2. • _____ invitamos a comer con nosotros, ¿qué decís?   las

   ○ ¿_____ invitáis de verdad? ¡Qué bien!   nos

3. • ¿Has visto las fotos de mi familia?   os

   ○ Sí, ya _____ he visto.   te

4. • ¿_____ han llamado hoy por teléfono?   lo

   ○ No, Rosita, no _____ ha llamado nadie.

◀ **todavía** — *still; yet*
¿qué decís?
(▶ **decir** — *to say*) —
what do you think?
nadie — *nobody,*
no one

cincuenta y siete | 57

*Numbers from 51 to 100 — Intercultural tip: **Don** and **Doña***

▶ § 38 Numbers

16

Now learn the numbers from 51 to 100. Listen to the numbers on the CD and repeat them.

Good to know:

Do you remember? The tens and the ones are written as separate words, starting with numbers over 30: **ochenta y tres, ochenta y cuatro, ochenta y cinco**.

cincuenta y uno   sesenta   sesenta y dos   setenta   setenta y tres

ochenta   noventa   cien

Good to know:

Telephone numbers can be given in different ways. A mixture of two-digit and single-digit numbers is quite common: 8-77-40 (**ocho — setenta y siete — cuarenta**).

17

Listen to five brief dialogues on the CD, and write down the telephone numbers that you hear. You can listen to the dialogues as often as you like. Can you give your own telephone number in Spanish?

18

As you already know, the familiar, or informal, pronoun **tú** (*you*) is very widely used in Spain. The polite, or formal, form **usted** is a sign of respect for older people or authority figures. Charo, for example, calls her mother-in-law **usted** to show respect. This usage is still common among the older generation today. But younger Spaniards address their in-laws with the informal **tú**.

The forms **Don** (*Mr.*) and **Doña** (*Mrs.*) are used in Spanish only with the first name. They are respectful terms of address, but generally they are used only with certain people. People who are over 45 use this form of address for older people, and older people use it among themselves as well.

Intercultural Tip

Fruits and vegetables — Days of the week — Statements of time

1

Look at the fruit and vegetable stand below. Listen to all the words and expressions on the CD and repeat them. Then match the translations with the appropriate Spanish words.

> **Good to know:**
> Make sure that statements of quantity always use the preposition **de** to link the terms:
> **un kilo de fresas,**
> **medio kilo de**
> **tomates**

a. *half a kilo of tomatoes*

c. *a kilo of strawberries*

d. *potatoes*

b. *pistachios*

i. *carrots*

e. *bananas*

g. *apples*

f. *heads of lettuce*

h. *peppers*

j. *oranges*

1. las naranjas
2. un kilo de fresas
3. los plátanos
4. las manzanas
5. los pimientos
6. medio kilo de tomates
7. las zanahorias
8. las lechugas
9. los pistachos
10. las patatas

2 TR. 68

Listen to the following days of the week and statements of time on the CD, and repeat each of them.

lunes	*Monday*
martes	*Tuesday*
miércoles	*Wednesday*
jueves	*Thursday*
viernes	*Friday*
sábado	*Saturday*
domingo	*Sunday*
por la mañana	*in the morning*
por la tarde	*in the afternoon/evening*
por la noche	*in the evening/at night*

> **Good to know:**
> The days of the week all are masculine and are written in lower case: **el lunes,**
> **el martes, …**

Noelia shops at the market

3

Noelia is shopping at the market. She runs into Chema there and makes a date with him. Listen to the dialogue on the CD and look at the pictures.

4

Here are a few questions about the dialogue between Noelia and Chema at the market. Answer the questions and mark the correct answers. If you need help in answering the questions, feel free to listen to the dialogue several times before doing the exercise.

1. ¿Qué compra Noelia además de manzanas?
   (*What else does Noelia buy besides apples?*)
   a. ■ naranjas y fresas
   b. ■ naranjas, plátanos y fresas
   c. ■ naranjas, pistachos y fresas

2. ¿Cuántas fresas compra Noelia?
   (*What amount of strawberries does Noelia buy?*)
   a. ■ un kilo y medio (1,5 kg.)
   b. ■ medio kilo (1/2 kg.)
   c. ■ un kilo (1 kg.)

3. ¿Cuánto es todo? (*How much does it all cost?*)
   a. ■ 13,50 euros   b. ■ 30,50 euros   c. ■ 13,15 euros

4. ¿Cuándo van a ir al cine Noelia y Chema?
   (*When are Noelia and Chema going to go to the movies?*)
   a. ■ el lunes por la noche
   b. ■ el lunes por la tarde
   c. ■ el domingo por la tarde

5. ¿A qué hora quedan? (*What time do they agree on?*)
   a. ■ a las seis   b. ■ a las diez   c. ■ a las nueve

Good to know:

The construction **ir** + **a** + infinitive refers to the near future: **Mañana voy a viajar a París**. (*Tomorrow I'm going to travel to Paris.*)

At the market

5 TR. 70

Noelia mentions a few things in the dialogue. Listen to the sentences on the CD as you read them. Then repeat them.

Quería un kilo de manzanas.

I'd like a kilo of apples.

¿Me pone medio kilo?

Can you give me half a kilo?

¿Cuánto es?

How much is it?

¿Puedo probarlas?

Can I taste them?

Bueno, aquí tiene.

Fine, here you are.
(literally: *Fine, here you have.*)

6 TR. 69 ✎

Now listen to the dialogue again and read along in the companion book. What do you say when you want to accept a suggestion? In the dialogue this is expressed in three ways. Find all three in the dialogue and write them in the balloons. Finally, you can read the translation of the entire dialogue in the companion book.

*The irregular verbs **poner**, **querer**, and **poder***

7

poner	
_____	ponemos
pones	ponéis
pone	ponen

▶ § 27 Indirect Object
   Pronouns

Good to know:

The verb **faltar** (*to be lacking; to be needed*) can also be used with an indirect object pronoun: **Me faltan algunas cosas**. (*I need a few things.*)

The verb **poner** (here: *to give*) occurs in the dialogue; **poner** is regular in the present tense, with the exception of the first person singular, **yo**.
Listen to the sound of the irregular form on the CD, and write it in the conjugation box at left.
In the dialogue, **poner** follows an indirect object pronoun (¿Qué **te** pongo?).
Do you remember all the forms? If not, you can look them up in the Grammar section.
Fill in the blanks below with the indirect object pronouns.

1. ¿Qué (*you*, pol. pl.) _____ pongo, señoras?

2. ¿ (*me*) _____ pones unas manzanas, Manolo?

3. ¿ (*us*) _____ pone dos cafés, por favor?

4. ¿ (*you*, fam. pl.) _____ falta algo, chicos?

8

el diseño —   ▶
drawing

▶ § 14 Irregular
   Verbs

The verbs **querer** (*to want*) and **poder** (*to be able; can; may*) are irregular verbs of the second conjugation (ending in **-er**). Look at the following sentences and underline the conjugated forms of the verbs **querer** and **poder**.

Lo siento, Chema, pero no puedo.
El lunes quiero terminar un diseño.

In both forms, the stem vowel undergoes a change (p**o**der ▶ p**ue**do; qu**e**rer ▶ qu**ie**ro). This change affects the forms that are stressed on the stem: qu**ie**ro, p**ue**do.
Now look at all the forms of **querer** and **poder** in the Grammar section.

Good to know:

The form **siento** in the expression **lo siento** (*I'm sorry*) comes from the verb **sentir**. The stem vowel of this verb changes (**e** ▶ **ie**) in the same way as the verb **querer**.

Fill in the blanks with the appropriate verb forms, and use the CD to check your answers.

> quieren — podéis — quieres — quieren

1. ¿ _____ tomar algo, Noelia?

2. Si ustedes _____ , _____ ver el piso hoy.

3. Chicos, ¿ _____ llamar a Chema, por favor?

9

In the dialogue at the market, Noelia says to Chema: **¡Hola, Chema! ¿Tú también de compras?** He answers her this way: **Sí ... hoy tengo que cocinar yo y me faltan algunas cosas.**

It is Chema's turn to cook today, and he expresses that by saying **tengo que cocinar**; thus **tener + que** (+ infinitive) means *to have to.*

1
TR. 73
Listen to three mini-dialogues on the CD and repeat the answers.

1. ¿Qué tienes que hacer hoy? — Hoy tengo que ir a la oficina.
2. ¿Qué tenéis que hacer ahora? — Tenemos que hablar con el jefe.
3. ¿Qué tal en la empresa? — Muy bien, pero tenemos que trabajar mucho.

10 TR. 74

Try to put these verb forms in the correct blanks, and then compare your answers with the sentences on the CD.

van — vas — va — vais

1. Yo voy mañana a la piscina. ¿Tú cuándo _____ ?

2. ¿Tu hija _____ a la universidad?

3. Nosotros vamos al museo del Prado. Y ustedes ¿ _____ al Retiro?

4. ¿Por qué no _____ al cine?

As you may already have guessed, the verb **ir** (*to go*) is irregular. Now fill in the missing forms of **ir** in the conjugation box at right.

ir	
_____	_____
vas	vais
va	van

11

Complete the dialogue with the verbs provided. If you need help with the irregular verbs, go to the Grammar section.

- Vosotros, ¿a qué hora *(ir)* _____ hoy al cine?

○ A las diez, pero antes *(tener)* _____ que comprar las entradas.

- ¿ *(poder)* _____ ir Carla y yo con vosotros?

○ ¿ *(querer)* _____ venir con nosotros? ¡Qué bien!

▶ § 14 Irregular Verbs

◀ **antes** — *before; also first*
la entrada — *ticket of admission*
venir — *to come*

Telling time — Making a date

12

Good to know:

In colloquial speech, the time of day is usually given in terms of the 12-hour clock (**a las tres**). In official statements of time, such as train time-tables, the 24-hour clock is used (**a las 15 horas**).

To ask the time, say **¿Qué hora es?** (*What time is it?*). On the CD, listen to ten dialogues in which a time of day is stated. Read the times and repeat them.

1. Es la una. (1.00)
2. Son las dos y cinco. (2.05)
3. Son las tres y diez. (3.10)
4. Son las cuatro y cuarto. (4.15)
5. Son las cinco y veinte. (5.20)
6. Son las seis y media. (6.30)
7. Son las siete menos veinticinco. (6.35)
8. Son las ocho menos veinte. (7.40)
9. Son las nueve menos cuarto. (8.45)
10. Son las diez en punto. (10.00)

As you see here, the form **es** (**Es la una**) is used for *It's one o'clock*, but starting with two o'clock, the form is **son** (**Son las dos**).

13

Good to know:

The sentence **Por favor, ¿tiene hora?** is a more formal way of asking the time of day.

Listen to five mini-dialogues on the CD. What times are mentioned in each of them? Write the appropriate number (1–5) under each clock face below.

14

Good to know:

The article must be used with the days of the week: **¿Quedamos el sábado?**

To make a date, you can use the verb **quedar** (here: *to agree on*). Listen to the following dialogue, and read along.

- Oye, ¿quedamos el sábado para tomar un café?
- Vale, ¿a qué hora?
- ¿Te va bien a las cinco y media?

The question **¿A qué hora?** (*At what time?*) can be answered with **A la una** (*At one o'clock*), **A la una y cuarto**, **A las dos**.

¿Te va bien a las seis menos cuarto?
Does that suit you, or would you like to suggest a different time?

Making a date — Numbers over 100

15

Agustín meets an old friend, Manolo, on the street and makes a date with him. Here you see a portion of their conversation, but the order has gotten mixed up. Put the sentences in the correct order and number them 1-8. Then listen to the entire dialogue between Agustín and Manolo on the CD, and compare.

◀ **salimos** ▶ **salir** — *to go out*
el compromiso — *date, appointment*
¿qué tal … ? — *what about … ?*
de acuerdo — *all right; agreed*
el barrio — *neighborhood*
la idea — *idea*

- ■ *Agustín:* ¿Os va bien a la una y media?
- ■ *Manolo:* Es una buena idea. Bueno, y ¿a qué hora quedamos?
- ■ *Agustín:* Podemos ir a comer al restaurante nuevo del barrio.
- ■ *Manolo:* Perfecto.
- ■ *Agustín:* Vale, pues quedamos el domingo a esa hora.
- ■ *Manolo:* ¿El domingo? De acuerdo.
- ■ *Agustín:* Lo siento, Manolo, mañana no podemos porque ya tenemos un compromiso pero, ¿qué tal el domingo?
- ■ *Manolo:* Oye, Agustín, ¿por qué no salimos mañana a cenar con las mujeres?

16

And more numbers! Listen to these on the CD, repeat them, and fill in the blanks below.

▶ § 38 Numbers

100 cien	600 _____	10.000 diez mil
101 ciento uno	700 setecientos	100.000 _____
200 doscientos	800 _____	1.000.000 un millón
300 trescientos	900 novecientos	2.000.000 dos millones
400 _____	1000 mil	3.000.000 tres _____
500 **quinientos**	2000 dos mil	1.000.000.000 mil millones

Good to know:
You need to use **y** only between the tens and the ones:
mil novecientos noventa y nueve (1999).

17

Do you remember the Spanish words for these fruits and vegetables? Write the weights given below in words and grams (**gramos**), as well as the type of fruit or vegetable: for example, **doscientos cuarenta y nueve gramos de tomates**.

Good to know:
Remember that statements of quantity always need to contain the preposition **de**.

1.197 Kg — I

0.856 Kg — 2

0,768 Kg — 3

2,525 Kg — 4

0,914 Kg — 5

sesenta y cinco | 65

Role play: At the market — Intercultural tip: Vocabulary differences

18

> **a ver** —*so; let's see* ▶
> **la ensalada** —
> *salad*
> **la lechuguita** —
> *small head of lettuce*
> (diminutive form)
> **¡cómo no!** — *of*
> *course! why not?*

Chema is at the market, doing some shopping. Listen to the conversation between Chema and the vendor. Then play the role of Chema and complete the dialogue.

> **Vendor:**   A ver, ¿qué te pongo?

You ask whether he has tomatoes: _____

> **Vendor:**   Por supuesto.

You would like one and one-half kilos of tomatoes: _____

> **Vendor:**   ¿Algo más?

You also would like half a kilo of carrots: _____

> **Vendor:**   Éstas están muy buenas. ¿Quieres una lechuga también?

You would rather have two: _____

> **Vendor:**   Pues dos lechuguitas.

You would also like strawberries and want to sample one:

_____

> **Vendor:**   ¡Claro, hombre! Están muy ricas. Son del país.

You would like 500 grams: _____

> **Vendor:**   ¡Cómo no!

You ask how much everything costs: _____

> **Vendor:**   Son 5 euros 30.

You give him the money, thank him, and say good-bye:

_____

19

If you think about the broad geographic distribution of the Spanish language and the 400 million speakers of Spanish, it's understandable that the Spanish lexicon exhibits not only regional differences within Spain itself, but also differences between Spain and Latin America, as well as within Latin America.

Here you see a few examples of terms for fruits and vegetables:

- **plátano** (*banana*) is **guineo** in Puerto Rico, **cambur** in Venezuela, and **banana** in Argentina.
- **cacahuete** (*peanut*) is **maní** almost everywhere in Latin America.
- **maíz** (*corn*) is called **choclo** in South America.
- **papa** (*potato*) is used in Latin America, Andalusia, and on the Canary Islands, while the rest of Spain says **patata**.
- In Mexico and Cuba, people say **frijoles** (*beans*), but in Puerto Rico the word is **habichuelas**, while they say **caraotas** in Venezuela and **porotos** in the rest of Latin America. In Spain, however, they are **alubias** or **judías**.

Intercultural Tip

Means of transportation — Statements of location

1 TR. 81

In this picture you see various means of transportation. Read the Spanish terms and listen to them on the CD. With the help of the pictures, you can surely guess their meanings. Listen to the words once more and repeat them.

Good to know:
Another word for **coche** (*car*) is **automóvil**. In Latin America, people also say **carro**.

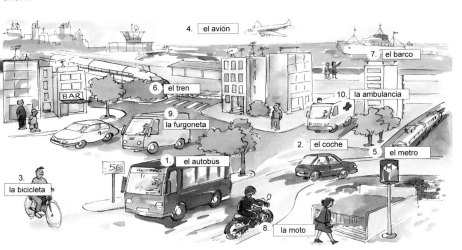

- 4. el avión
- 7. el barco
- 6. el tren
- 10. la ambulancia
- 9. la furgoneta
- 2. el coche
- 5. el metro
- 1. el autobús
- 3. la bicicleta
- 8. la moto

2 TR. 82 🖉

¿Dónde está nuestro coche? *(Where is our car?)*
Look at the pictures, read the sentences, and listen to them on the CD as well. Then write the English translations for the statements of place in the vocabulary box below.

Good to know:
Del is a contraction of the preposition **de** and the article **el**. The same thing happens with the preposition **a** + the article **el** ▶ **al**: ¿Vamos **al** restaurante?

El coche está a la derecha de la bicicleta.

El coche está a la izquierda del taxi.

El coche está enfrente de la parada de autobús.

El coche está delante del coche de bomberos.

El coche está detrás de la furgoneta.

◀ **la parada** — *stop (bus, etc.)* **el coche de bomberos** — *fire truck*

a la derecha — _____

a la izquierda — _____

enfrente — _____

delante — _____

detrás — _____

Rosita has a date — Giving directions

3

Rosita has a date in a restaurant. At home, she asks Jordi and Chema the best way to get there. Look at the pictures and listen to the dialogue several times.

Don't worry if you don't always understand everything! Concentrate on familiar things and take advantage of the pictures; with their help, you can imagine the context of the dialogue much more clearly.

4

Listen to these directions on the CD and try to repeat the sentences. Then look at the translation.

¿Cómo quieres ir, en metro o en autobús?	*How do you intend to go, by subway or by bus?*
Tienes que bajar en la parada Tribunal y tomar la salida Fuencarral.	*You have to get out at the Tribunal stop and take the Fuencarral exit.*
Luego sigues todo recto por Fuencarral y giras a la derecha en la tercera bocacalle.	*Then go straight ahead on Fuencarral and turn right at the third cross street.*

Giving directions — Correcting yourself

5

Indicate whether the following statements are true (**correcto**) or false (**falso**). You can listen to the dialogue as often as you wish. In the vocabulary box on the right, you will find the new words you need.

◀ **la dirección** — *address*
el lugar — *place*
lejos — *far*
la línea de metro — *subway line*
el compañero — *colleague*

		correcto	falso
1.	Rosita tiene que ir al museo.		
2.	La dirección es calle Colón, número 76.		
3.	El lugar no está muy lejos.		
4.	Rosita quiere ir en metro.		
5.	La línea de metro es directa desde su casa.		
6.	Rosita ha quedado con un compañero de trabajo.		
7.	Rosita ha quedado a las ocho de la tarde.		
8.	Chema cree que Rosita ha quedado con un amigo.		

6

Now listen to the dialogue again while you read along in the companion book. What do you say if you need to correct yourself? Write this expression in the balloon below.

Four times in this dialogue, there occurs an expression meaning that someone has to do something. Underline the four expressions in the dialogue. If you like, you can conclude by reading the translation of the dialogue in the companion book.

*Irregular verbs: **Conocer** and **decir** — Prepositions: **A** and **en***

7

conocer	
conozco	_____
_____	_____
_____	_____

The verb **conocer** (*to know*), with the exception of the first person singular, is a regular verb ending in -**er**, like **comer**. Listen to the irregular form on the CD, repeat it, and then write the missing regular forms of **conocer** in the conjugation box on the left. The first person singular of **decir** (*to say*) is also irregular: **Yo digo**. The vowel in the stem **dec-** changes to **dic-** when the stress falls on the first syllable. Here you see all the forms of **decir**:

yo digo	nosotros / nosotras decimos
tú <u>dices</u>	vosotros / vosotras decís
él / ella / usted <u>dice</u>	ellos / ellas / ustedes <u>dicen</u>

8

Fill in the blanks in these mini-dialogues with the appropriate verb forms.

Good to know:
In the case of the verb **seguir**, the vowel in **seg-** changes to **sig-** when the stem is stressed (as with **decir**): **sigo** / **digo**; **seguimos** / **decimos**.

1. ● ¿ (*you fam. pl./know*) _____ a mi hermano?

    ○ Pues claro que lo (*we/know*) _____ .

2. ● Perdona, ¿qué (*you fam. sing./say*) _____ ?

    (*I/say*) _____ que (*we/have to*) _____ que irnos.

3. ● Oye, ¿cómo (*we/can*) _____ llegar al centro?

    ○ Es muy fácil. (*you fam. pl./follow*) _____ esta calle y (*you fam. pl./cross*) _____ la plaza. (*you fam. pl./take*) _____ _____ la segunda bocacalle y después (*you fam. pl./turn*) _____ a la izquierda.

9

§ 37 Prepositions

The verb **ir** means both *to walk* and *to ride*, and it is used to indicate the means of transportation in the construction **ir + en** . . . :
    Yo voy al trabajo <u>en coche</u>.

However, **ir a pie** (*to go on foot, to walk*) is an exception:
    Mi casa no está lejos. Podemos ir <u>a pie</u>.

How do you get to work? **¿Cómo va usted al trabajo?**
Give an answer, using the expressions **en coche**, **en bicicleta**, **en autobús**, **a pie**.

Prepositions — Times of day

10

Which words are missing here? Complete the sentences, and compare your answers with the correct answers on the CD.

▶ § 37 Prepositions

    1. Voy _____ un restaurante en la calle Colón.

    2. El restaurante está _____ la calle Colón.

    3. La abuela no está _____ casa.

    4. ¡Tengo mucho sueño! Me voy _____ la cama.

The preposition **a** is used to express direction (with or without an article, depending on the situation):

    Mañana tengo que ir <u>a</u> la oficina. / ¿Queréis ir <u>al</u> cine?
    ¿Vamos <u>a</u> casa / <u>a</u> Sevilla?

The preposition **a** always is placed between **ir** and an infinitive:

    Voy a cenar. / Vamos a bailar.

As you already know, **estar en** is used to indicate location: **El piso está <u>en</u> el Paseo de la Castellana.**

Good to know:
When you visit some-one, you also use **ir a casa**: **Voy a casa de Chema. ¿Vamos a casa de los primos?**

11

You are already aware that in colloquial speech, the 12-hour clock is used for telling time. To specify the time of day if it is not apparent from the context, you need to add **de la mañana, de la tarde, de la noche.**
Listen to the following times and repeat them.

Son las diez y cuarto de la mañana.   Son las cinco y media de la tarde.   Son las once menos cuarto de la noche.

If you mention times of day without reference to a particular hour, you should use **por**: **¿Trabajas también <u>por</u> la tarde?**

Giving directions — Prepositions

12

You are somewhere in Spain and want to get directions.
This is how you can address passersby:

> **Oiga, perdone, . . .** (you, pol. sing.)   **Perdón, . . .**
> **Oye, perdona, . . .** (you, fam. sing.)   **Por favor, . . .**

Then you can formulate your question this way:
¿Sabe dónde está la Plaza Mayor?
¿Sabes si hay una farmacia por aquí cerca? *(a pharmacy nearby)*

The answer could contain the following expressions:
> **Tiene que ...** *(You have to ...; pol.)*   **Tienes que ...** *(You have to ...; fam.)*
> **bajar en la parada Tribunal**
> **tomar la primera** *(first)* / **segunda** *(second)* / **tercera** *(third)* **calle**
> **seguir** *(keep going)* **todo recto hasta el semáforo** *(traffic light)*
> **torcer** / **girar** / **doblar** *(turn)* **a la derecha** /
> **a la izquierda en la primera bocacalle**
> **cruzar** *(cross)* **la calle** / **la plaza** *(square)*

TR. 88   Now listen to the dialogue on the CD. What are they trying to find?

13 🖉

Fill in the blanks with the missing prepositions.

> 1. ¿Cómo vas _____ la oficina? ¿ _____ pie o _____ metro?
>
> 2. ¿Sabéis si la biblioteca está _____ la calle Alcalá?
>
> 3. ¿El ayuntamiento está enfrente _____ bar o _____ lado?
>
> 4. El autobús circula desde las seis _____ la mañana. _____ la noche
>   no hay servicio.
>
> 5. • _____ favor, ¿hay un estanco _____ aquí cerca?
>
>   ○ Sí, tiene que girar _____ la derecha y seguir _____ el semáforo.

la biblioteca —
library
el ayuntamiento
— *town hall*
circular — *to go*
around, to travel
el servicio — *service*
el estanco — *tobacco*
store

Good to know:

In a Spanish **estanco**
(tobacco store), you
can buy not only to-
bacco products, but
also **sellos** *(stamps)*
and **periódicos**
(newspapers).

Stress and written accents — Interrogatives

14 🖉

Fill in the blanks below with the correct form of the definite or definite article — if one is needed at all.

1. • Perdone, ¿dónde está _____ catedral?

   ○ Detrás de _____ Plaza Mayor.

2. • Oye, perdona, ¿dónde hay _____ parada de taxi?

   ○ Delante del parque.

3. • Perdón, ¿hay _____ banco por aquí cerca?

   ○ Sí, está entre _____ cine y _____ Correos.

4. • ¿Sabe dónde está _____ hotel "Reconquista"?

   ○ Sí, está en _____ Plaza Mayor.

15 👓

Some words bear a written accent because they do not follow the stress rules of Spanish. However, a written accent is also used

- to distinguish all interrogatives:
  ¿Qué? *(What?)*   **¿Quién?** *(Who?)*   **¿Cómo?** *(How?)*
  ¿Dónde? *(Where?)*   **¿De dónde?** *(From where?)*   **¿Adónde?** *(To where?)*
  These words bear a written accent in indirect questions as well, for example:
  Noelia no sabe dónde está la abuela.

- to distinguish certain one-syllable words from others spelled and pronounced the same way:
  tú *(you)*   **tu** *(your)*   **sé** *(I know)*   **se** (reflexive pronoun)
  él *(he)*   **el** *(the)*   **sí** *(yes)*   **si** *(if, whether)*
  té *(tea)*   **te** *(you; direct and indirect object pronoun)*

🖉

Look at the following sentences and add the missing accents.

1. ¿Como se llama tu mujer?
2. Yo no se donde vive el; y ¿tu?

▶ **§ 3 Stress and Written Accents**

▶ **§ 36 Interrogatives**

Good to know:
The interrogative **¿quiénes?** is the plural form of **¿quién?** *(who?)*. Compare: **¿Quién es usted? ¿Quiénes son ustedes?**

Good to know:
Adding the plural ending **-es** can cause a word to lose or gain a written accent, in order to preserve the stress: **catalán–catalanes, joven–jóvenes**.

Story in pictures — Game: Guess the letters — Intercultural tip: Spanish addresses

16

These pictures are out of order. Listen to the dialogue and then put the pictures in the correct order by numbering them from 1–6. Then you can listen to the dialogue again while you read the text in the companion book.

17

Another little game: Guess the missing words. Have fun!

1. *To walk:* __ _ ___

2. *A business:* ___ _____

3. *Ask how someone gets to work:* ¿____ ___ __ _____?

4. *To take a means of transportation:* __ __ _____

5. *A time:* _ ___ ____

18

When someone gives an address (la dirección), the name of the street is stated first, and then the number of the house or building. Various abbreviations are in use:

Montserrat Ulecia Pérez
C/ Mercadal 49, 1º izqda.
26500 Calahorra (La Rioja)

Tel.: 941 723 865

Calle (*Street*) is shortened to **C/**,
Avenida (*Avenue*) becomes **Avda.**,
Plaza (*Square or Place*) is abbreviated as **Pza.**,
sin número (*no number*) is **s / n**,
escalera (*staircase/stairwell*) is **esc.**,
derecha (*on the right*) is **dcha.**, and
izquierda (*on the left*) is **izqda.**

If you want to visit someone in Spain, it is important to know not only the street name and building number, but also the number and letter of the apartment, since occupants' names are usually not displayed at the building entrance.

Intercultural tip

Gift items — Sports

1 TR. 90

In the pictures below, you see a few typical gift items. Listen to the Spanish words on the CD and repeat them.

un ramo
de flores

cosméticos

una caja de
bombones

unos patines
en línea

un libro

un casco
protector

joyas y bisutería

ropa

2 TR. 91

The people in this picture are very active and are participating in a number of sports. Read the Spanish words for the various sports, listen to them on the CD, and repeat them.

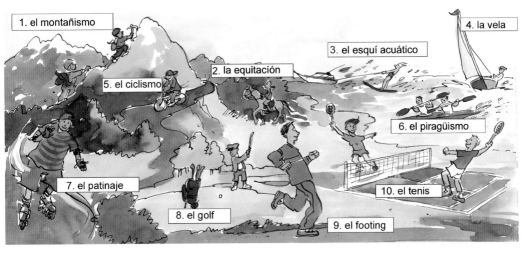

1. el montañismo
4. la vela
3. el esquí acuático
2. la equitación
5. el ciclismo
6. el piragüismo
7. el patinaje
10. el tenis
8. el golf
9. el footing

Chema and Rosita buy a present for Noelia

3 TR. 92

Chema and his apartment mate Rosita are at a shopping center. Rosita is supposed to help Chema find an appropriate birthday present for Noelia. Look at the pictures and listen to the dialogue on the CD.

4 TR. 93

Listen to the following sentences on the CD and repeat them. Then look at the translations.

¿Le gustan los cosméticos? ¡A mí me encantan!

No me atrevo a comprárselos.

¿Cómo es su carácter, qué le gusta?

Tiene una elegancia natural, no sé cómo decirte.

¿Qué tal si le compramos unos patines en línea?

Does she like cosmetics? I adore them!

I don't trust myself to buy them for her.

What is her personality like, what does she like?

She has a natural elegance, I don't know how to explain it to you.

How about if we buy her some inline skates?

Buying gifts

5

Listen to the entire dialogue and answer the following questions by marking the correct answers.

◀ **personal** —
personal
prefiere ▶ **preferir**
— *to prefer*
practicar — *to go in for*
el motociclismo —
motorcycle sports
el perfume —
perfume
cuesta ▶ **costar** —
to cost
el regalo — *gift, present*
el color — *color*

I. ¿Por qué Chema no le compra cosméticos?
a. ■ porque a ella no le gustan
b. ■ porque es una cosa muy personal
c. ■ porque no sabe qué cosmético prefiere

2. ¿Qué le gusta a Noelia?
a. ■ la bisutería
b. ■ las joyas
c. ■ la ropa moderna

3. ¿Qué deporte practica Noelia?
a. ■ el motociclismo
b. ■ el patinaje
c. ■ el footing

4. ¿Qué quieren comprar Chema y Rosita?
a. ■ un perfume
b. ■ un casco protector
c. ■ unos patines en línea

5. ¿Cuánto cuesta el regalo que compran?
a. ■ € 85,50
b. ■ € 150
c. ■ € 58,50

6. ¿Qué le gusta a Rosita del regalo?
a. ■ el color
b. ■ el precio
c. ■ la calidad

Good to know:
Amounts involving cents can be expressed with **con** or with **y**: € 6.80 =
seis euros con ochenta céntimos /
seis euros y ochenta céntimos.

6

Listen to the entire dialogue once more while reading it in the companion book. How does Chema ask Rosita's opinion? Find the question in the dialogue and write it in the balloon below.

If you like, now you can look at the translation of the dialogue in the companion book.

*The verb **costar** — The interrogative **cuánto** — Demonstratives*

7

Good to know:

Besides **¿Cuánto cuesta(n)?**, you can also ask the price by saying **¿Qué precio tiene?**, as here:
¿Qué precio tiene este casco protector?
¿Qué precio tienen estos patines?

The verb **costar** (*to cost*) is irregular (**o ▶ ue**). It is used in the third person to inquire about the price of an item: **¿Cuánto cuesta?**
Listen to the following dialogue between a customer and a saleswoman. Then play the role of the customer and complete the dialogue.

Customer:	_____
Saleswoman:	150 euros.
Customer:	_____
Saleswoman:	Los patines cuestan 200 euros.

8

▶ § 36 Interrogatives

Good to know:

The interrogative **cuánto** agrees with the noun to which it refers:
Quería unas fresas.
— Sí, ¿cuántas?

Fill in the blanks with the correct interrogatives.

cuántos — cuánta — cuántas — cuánto

1. ¡_____ ropa tienes! — Es que me encanta ir de compras.

2. ¿_____ dinero tienes? — Tengo 15 euros, ¿y tú?

3. ¡_____ flores!, ¡y qué bonitas son! — Me las ha regalado mi vecino.

4. Y tú, ¿_____ años tienes? — Tengo 25 años.

9

▶ § 33 Demonstratives

Good to know:

A written accent on the pronoun is required in order to prevent misunderstanding:
Dice que ésta (*a woman*) **mañana no tiene tiempo**.
Otherwise, the written accent is optional.
Eso / esto, however, never bear a written accent.

As you already know, the forms **este / esta / estos / estas** (*this / these*) designate certain objects or persons who are in the immediate vicinity of the speaker.
The demonstratives **ese / esa / esos / esas** (*that / those*) however, refer to objects or persons that are farther away from the speaker.

Both forms can be used alone or in combination with a noun, with which they must agree in gender and number.
¿Cuánto cuesta este casco? — ¿Éste? 85 euros con 50.

The form **eso** (just like **esto**) refers to something that is not specified (neuter) and always stands alone:
Es una persona abierta y eso me gusta.

Demonstratives — Stressed indirect object pronouns

10 ✎

▶ § 33 Demonstratives

Look at the pictures and fill in the blanks with the correct demonstratives
(**esta / este / estas / estos** or **esa / ese / esas / esos**).

◀ **rojo / a** — *red*

1. _____ libro es muy interesante.

2. ¿Cuánto cuestan _____ flores?

3. _____ señora de la foto es tu madre, ¿no?

4. ¿Te gustan _____ zapatos rojos?

5. ¿Por qué no le compramos _____ casco?

11 👓

In Spanish, the indirect object pronoun (*me, you*, etc.) can occur twice. In
addition to the unstressed pronouns (**me, te, le, nos, os, les**), the stressed
pronouns can be used as well: **A mí me encantan los cosméticos.**
In place of the stressed pronoun, there may be a name in the sentence:
¿A Noelia le gustan los cosméticos?
This repetition serves to emphasize the person and avoid misunderstan-
dings (especially in the third person, since **le** can mean *him, her*, or *you* and
les can mean *them* or *you*.

▶ § 27 Indirect Object Pronouns

Here you see all the stressed pronouns:

a mí	**a nosotros / a nosotras**
a ti	**a vosotros / a vosotras**
a él / a ella / a usted	**a ellos / a ellas / a ustedes**

Good to know:
Note that **mí** requires
a written accent to
distinguish it from the
form **mi** (*my*).

TR. 95 ✎

Fill in the blanks with the stressed indirect object pronouns, and use the CD
to check your answers.

> a ustedes — a vosotros — a mí — a ellas — a ti — a nosotros — a él

1. ¿ _____ te falta algo?

2. _____ no le gustan los museos, pero a mí sí.

3. _____ nos gusta mucho viajar.

4. _____ os encanta el cine, ¿verdad?

Indirect object pronouns after prepositions — Combined pronouns

12

§ 27 Indirect Object Pronouns

With prepositions such as **para** (*for*), **con** (*with*), and **sin** (*without*), the same stressed pronouns are used as with **a: Este regalo es para ti.**

Translate the expressions given in parentheses into Spanish, and write them in the appropriate blanks.

1. ¿Este ramo de flores es (*for me*) _____?

2. Ana trabaja (*with you* pol. sing.) _____, ¿verdad?

3. Si queréis, podéis ir (*without me*) _____.

4. (*without you* fam. sing.) _____, no vamos a la fiesta.

With the preposition **con**, the first and second persons singular are irregular: **conmigo** (*with me*), **contigo** (*with you*).
¿Quieres venir conmigo? / Me encanta trabajar contigo.

13

§ 28 Combined Pronouns

If both an indirect and a direct object pronoun are used in a sentence, the indirect object pronoun precedes the direct one. Both precede the verb:

- ¿Te gusta mi bicicleta?
- Sí, mucho.
- ¡Pues te la regalo!

The indirect object pronouns **le / les** become **se** if followed by **lo / la / los / las.**

- ¿Le has comprado ya a tu madre el regalo?
- No, todavía no se lo he comprado.

14

Fill in the blanks in the following dialogue with the correct pronouns.

1. • ¿Quién te ha regalado estas flores?

   ○ _____ _____ ha regalado un amigo.

2. • ¿Le habéis comprado la bufanda a la abuela?

   ○ Sí, _____ _____ hemos comprado esta tarde.

3. • ¿Quién os ha regalado los patines?

   ○ _____ _____ han regalado los tíos.

15

In infinitive constructions with verbs such as **querer**, **poder** or constructions like **tener que** + infinitive, the pronouns can precede the verb or be attached to it:

> **Hola, buenos días. ¿<u>Les</u> puedo ayudar en algo?**
> **Hola, buenos días. ¿Puedo ayudar<u>les</u> en algo?**

 Change these sentences by attaching the pronouns to the end of the verb.

1. Te quiero regalar este libro.   2. Os tengo que decir una cosa.

With attached pronouns, the stress should remain on the same syllable of the verb; that is, if two pronouns are appended, a written accent must always be added: **No me atrevo a comprárselos.**

> **§ 29 Position of Pronouns**

> **Good to know:**
> Note that the pronouns are directly attached to the infinitive.

16

Listen to six sentences on the CD. Rewrite them by attaching the pronouns to the end of the infinitive, as here: **No te lo puedo decir ▶ No puedo decírtelo.** Remember to add the accent!

> **Good to know:**
> Colors are masculine: **el (color) blanco**. They agree with the noun they modify: **los coches azules**. The colors **naranja** and **rosa**, however, are invariable: **el casco rosa**.

17

Look at the rainbow and the Spanish words for the colors. Listen to them on the CD and repeat them.

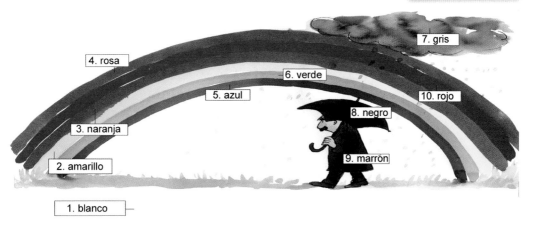

7. gris
4. rosa
6. verde
5. azul
8. negro
10. rojo
3. naranja
9. marrón
2. amarillo
1. blanco

Game: Bingo — Intercultural tip: Business hours in Spain

18

Would you like to play bingo? The CD will dictate various words to you. As soon as you hear a word that you see depicted on your bingo card, mark it. Once you have three marks in a row (horizontally, vertically, or diagonally), you have **¡Bingo!** But no cheating! Check the transcription in the companion book to see whether you really did mark the correct pictures.

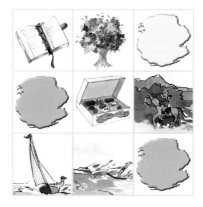

19

Business hours in Spain vary quite a lot. Smaller stores normally open from Monday through Saturday between 10 and 1:30 and in the afternoon from 4:30 or 5 to 8 or even 9 P.M.

Larger stores or stores in the center of town often do not take a midday break, and others even stay open round the clock.

The **centros comerciales** (*shopping centers*), **grandes almacenes** (*department stores*), and **hipermercados** (*very large supermarkets*) are open continuously from 10 A.M. until 10 P.M., including Saturdays.

Banks and post offices are usually open to the public Monday through Saturday from 8:30 A.M. to 2 P.M. Visits to the public authorities as a rule can be made from Monday through Friday between 8:30 and 2.

 Listen to the mini-dialogue on the CD, and find out where the person is going at the end.

Questions and answers — Giving directions

1

Which answer doesn't fit? Mark it with an X.

1. ¿Tienes que hacer algo mañana?
a. ■ Sí, quiero ir al centro para comprar una mesa.
b. ■ He estado con mis amigos.
c. ■ Tengo que terminar el proyecto.
d. ■ Pues, no; podemos hacer algo, si quieres.

2. ¿Tú sabes dónde está la parada de autobús?
a. ■ Sí, delante del cine.
b. ■ Creo que está enfrente del parque.
c. ■ Vive cerca de la estación.
d. ■ Al lado del supermercado hay una.

3. Perdone, ¿qué precio tienen estos zapatos?
a. ■ Un momento, por favor, ahora se lo digo.
b. ■ ¿Ésos? 44 euros.
c. ■ Cuestan 63 euros.
d. ■ Los quiero en negro.

4. ¿Tiene hora, por favor?
a. ■ Sí, es la una y media.
b. ■ No, lo siento.
c. ■ A las once y cuarto.
d. ■ Son las ocho menos veinte.

5. ¿Cómo quieres viajar?
a. ■ ¡Qué moto más bonita!
b. ■ En coche.
c. ■ Mejor en autobús.
d. ■ Creo que en tren es más rápido.

2

These pictures are out of order. Listen to the dialogue and put them back in the right order by numbering them from 1 to 6.

◀ **La Oficina de Información y Turismo**
— Tourist Information Office

Answering questions

3

Match the Spanish sentences on the right with the corresponding para-phrases on the left. Then check your answers by listening to the CD, and repeat the sentences.

la corbata — ▶
(neck)tie

1. *expressing an opinion*

2. *introducing an explanation*

3. *speaking to someone and asking for directions*

4. *buying something at the market*

5. *asking for something in the department store*

6. *making a suggestion*

7. *apologizing*

8. *asking for an opinion*

a. ¿Quedamos el viernes para ir al cine?

b. ¿Me puede enseñar alguna corbata en marrón?

c. Lo siento mucho, no he podido llegar en punto.

d. ¿Qué te parece este bolso rojo?

e. Hoy no puedo salir. Es que tengo que trabajar, ¿sabes?

f. ¡Tu idea me parece estupenda!

g. Quería medio kilo de fresas.

h. Oiga, perdone, ¿sabe si hay una farmacia por aquí cerca?

4

Answer the following questions, and try to use the words you've learned. If you need help, use the glossary in the back of the companion book.

1. ¿Qué le gusta hacer después de trabajar?
2. ¿Qué productos compra usted en el mercado?
3. ¿Cómo va al trabajo?

5

Read the following questions and answer them. The companion book contains some suggested answers.

1. ¿Qué deporte/s practica usted?
2. ¿Cómo es usted? ¿Qué carácter tiene?
3. ¿Qué color le gusta más?
4. ¿Qué hace usted para divertirse?
5. ¿A qué hora cena?
6. ¿Qué le han regalado en su último cumpleaños?
7. ¿Qué película ha visto en el cine recientemente?
8. ¿Qué ha hecho esta semana?

Irregular Verbs — **muy** and **mucho**

6

Do you remember these irregular verbs? Write the missing forms in the table.

▶ §14 Irregular Verbs

querer	poder	decir
		digo
quieres		dices
	puede	
queremos	podemos	
		decís

The stem vowel of these verbs changes in the forms that are stressed on the stem:

e ▸ ie: qu<u>e</u>rer ▸ qu<u>ie</u>ro   o ▸ ue: p<u>o</u>der ▸ p<u>ue</u>des   e ▸ i: d<u>e</u>cir ▸ d<u>i</u>go

7

Complete the following sentences, using the present tense forms of the verbs in parentheses. If you need help with the irregular verbs, go to the Grammar section.

▶ §14 Irregular Verbs

1. Oye, Jordi, ¿(*tener*) _____ que hacer algo mañana?

2. ¿Cuánto (*costar*) _____ estos zapatos?

3. ¿Cuánto le (*poner*) _____, señora?

4. Tú (*seguir*) _____ por aquí, y, al final, está el teatro.

5. Perdone, ¿(*haber*) _____ una farmacia por aquí cerca?

6. Yo no (*conocer*) _____ a esa persona, ¿y tú?

8

Fill in the blanks below with **muy** or **mucho**.

▶ §12 muy / mucho

1. Ese chico es simpático y _____ inteligente.

2. A nosotros nos gusta _____ hacer montañismo.

3. Esa raqueta me parece _____ cara.

◀ **la raqueta** — *tennis racquet*

4. Usted habla _____ bien el español.

Pronouns

9

> **§ 27 Indirect Object Pronouns**

Here you see four mini-dialogues. Fill in the blanks with the appropriate combinations of prepositions and pronouns. Pay attention to the context, and then use the CD to check your answers.

> sin vosotros — para mí — a ti — conmigo — para ti — sin ti — contigo — a mí

    1. • Oye, quería hablar _____ un momento.

      ○ ¿_____? Está bien.

    2. • He comprado este libro _____ .

      ○ ¿_____? ¡Qué amable eres!

    3. • Oye, Jordi, ¿_____ te han dicho algo del nuevo proyecto?

      ○ No, _____ nadie me ha dicho nada.

    4. • No quiero ir _____ .

      ○ Y nosotros _____ tampoco.

10

> **§ 28 Combined Object Pronouns**

Complete the following mini-dialogues by placing the direct and indirect object pronouns in the correct blanks. Use the CD to check your answers, and repeat the sentences out loud. Be careful! You will not need to use all the pronouns. If you need help, go to the Grammar section.

> le — me — te — os — los — la — les — se — las — nos — lo — se

    1. • ¿Por qué no me decís quién es?

      ○ No _____ _____ podemos decir todavía.

    2. • ¿Quién os ha regalado estas gafas?

      ○ _____ _____ ha regalado nuestra abuela.

    3. • ¿Le has dado la agenda a la secretaria?

      ○ Sí, _____ _____ he dado esta mañana.

    4. • ¿Les habéis comprado los regalos a vuestros padres?

      ○ Sí, _____ _____ hemos comprado hoy.

Prepositions — The present perfect

11 ✏

Look at the sentences below. Which preposition is needed to complete the sentence? Select the correct preposition for each.

▶ § 37 Prepositions

1. _____ la tarde he quedado con unos amigos. (*de/a/por*)

2. Yo siempre viajo _____ coche. (*en/con/a*)

3. En la primera bocacalle tienes que girar _____ la izquierda. (*de/por/a*)

4. Son las diez _____ la mañana. (*a/de/por*)

12 ✏

In the passage below, Rosita tells you what she has done today. Fill in the blanks with the appropriate verb in the present perfect. If you would like to review the formation of the present perfect, read the corresponding chapter in the Grammar.

▶ § 15 Present Perfect

Hoy por la mañana _____ unas compras en el centro. Después, a

mediodía, _____ en un restaurante y _____ un café en una

terraza. Luego _____ en el museo y _____ hasta las ocho.

Después _____ al supermercado y _____ una lechuga.

Mi madre me _____ por teléfono, ¡y las dos _____

hasta las once de la noche!

_____ una ensalada, _____ un poco la televisión y

ahora me voy a la cama.

¡Hasta mañana!

> **Good to know:**
> Some verbs have irregular past participles:
> **ver ▶ visto** (*seen*)
> **hacer ▶ hecho** (*made, done*)

13 ✏

Fill in the blanks with the present perfect form of the verbs given in parentheses.

1. Yo a ellos no les (*decir*) _____ nada.

2. Y tú, ¿qué (*hacer*) _____ este fin de semana?

3. La secretaria (*ser*) _____ muy amable con nosotros.

4. Y vosotros, ¿(*ver*) _____ esa película también?

Telling time — Statements of quantity, frequency, and place

14

On the CD, you will hear three mini-dialogues dealing with each picture below. Which dialogue matches the time shown on the clock? Mark the correct answer.

A

B

C

A	B	C
▨ Dialogue 1	▨ Dialogue 1	▨ Dialogue 1
▨ Dialogue 2	▨ Dialogue 2	▨ Dialogue 2
▨ Dialogue 3	▨ Dialogue 3	▨ Dialogue 3

15

Arrange the terms below in descending order, depending on their meaning, from more to less and from more frequent to less frequent.

poco — demasiado — bastante — nada — mucho

nunca — siempre — a veces — muchas veces

16

Match the sentences on the right with the appropriate pictures.

1.

a. Chema está enfrente de Jordi.

2.

b. Rosita está a la izquierda de Chema.

3.

c. Rosita está a la derecha de Jordi.

Numbers — A postcard from Madrid

17

Listen to the lucky numbers in the lottery and write them down.

18

With the help of the English words given here, fill in the blanks in the post-card that Rosita is writing to her friend.

> *(for) her — isn't it? — Tuesday — gift — very much — help —*
> *nice, kind — city*

¡Hola, Lupita!

¿Cómo estás? Madrid es una _____ muy bonita y me gusta

_____ trabajar en el museo.

Jordi y Chema, mis compañeros de piso, son unos chicos muy

_____ ; siempre me _____ en todo, ¡incluso

cocinan!

Este _____ he ido con Chema a comprar un regalo de cumple-

años para Noelia, la vecina.

Al final _____ hemos comprado un casco protector porque a

ella le encanta patinar. Un _____ muy original,

¿_____?

Un beso, Rosita

Intonation — Stress and written accents

19

For each item below, you will hear three sentences. As you listen, pay close attention to the intonation. Which of the three utterances is a question? Mark the questions. The pictures will help you understand the statements or questions.

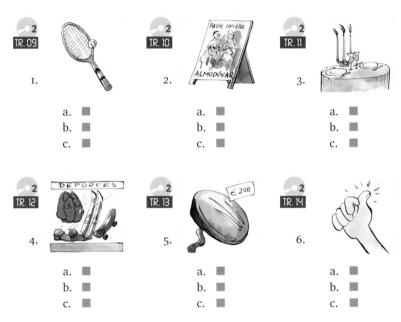

1.   TR. 09
- a. ▪
- b. ▪
- c. ▪

2.   TR. 10   *Hable con ella* / ALMODÓVAR
- a. ▪
- b. ▪
- c. ▪

3.   TR. 11
- a. ▪
- b. ▪
- c. ▪

4.   TR. 12   DEPORTES
- a. ▪
- b. ▪
- c. ▪

5.   TR. 13   € 208
- a. ▪
- b. ▪
- c. ▪

6.   TR. 14
- a. ▪
- b. ▪
- c. ▪

20

The accents are missing in the following sentences! Write in the missing accents.

1. ¿Donde trabaja tu marido?

2. Si quereis, podemos tomar te.

3. Tu no sabes quien es el, pero yo si lo se.

> It is best to always memorize a word and its appropriate accent at the same time.

21   TR. 15

The CD will dictate four sentences to you. Write them down, and don't forget to supply written accents wherever they are needed.

Beverages — The present participle

1

Look at these beverages. Which of them do you like to drink? Underline your favorite drinks.

un vino blanco   un vino tinto   un vino rosado   un vaso de leche   una caña de cerveza

un mosto   un refresco   agua sin gas   agua con gas   un zumo de naranja

2

Look at what these people are doing right now. Try to match the expressions with the people and number them from 1 to 8. Now, can you match the translations with the Spanish sentences?

■ está cortando cebolla — ■ están comiendo — ■ está viendo la televisión — ■ está llamando por teléfono — ■ está leyendo el periódico — ■ está enseñando un nuevo programa — ■ está preparando la cena — ■ están durmiendo

■ a. *she is making a telephone call*   ■ b. *they are eating*

■ c. *they are sleeping*   ■ d. *she is watching television*

■ e. *he is slicing onions*   ■ f. *he is reading the newspaper*

■ g. *he is teaching a new (computer) program*   ■ h. *she is preparing dinner*

Conversation between Charo and Agustín

3

It is evening: Mr. and Mrs. Giménez (Charo and Agustín) are at home. They are talking about Rosita, the new neighbor.
Look at the pictures and listen to the dialogue.

4 TR. 17

Here you see some sentences from the previous dialogue. Listen to them on the CD and repeat them. Then read the translations below.

> **Good to know:**
>
> The verb **tener** is used in many expressions, such as **tener hambre / sed** (*to be hungry / thirsty*), **tener frío / calor** (*to be cold / hot*), **tener prisa** (*to be in a hurry*), **tener 20 años** (*to be 20 years old*), **tener sueño** (*to be sleepy*).

1. ¡Estoy preparando algo de cena! ¿No tienes hambre?

2. Aquí tienes el cuchillo. ¿Puedes cortar las cebollas también?

3. A ti Chema te cae muy bien, ¿verdad?

4. El chico le está enseñando un nuevo programa de ordenador.

5. Se llevan muy bien los dos … ¿Puedes preguntarle si quiere cenar con nosotros?

a. *I'm making something for dinner! Aren't you hungry?*

b. *Here you have the knife. Can you slice the onions too?*

c. *You like Chema, don't you?*

d. *The boy is teaching her a new computer program.*

e. *The two of them get along very well … Can you ask him whether he wants to have dinner with us?*

Fixing dinner

5

Are the following statements true or false? Mark your answer. In the vocabulary box on the right, you'll find help with the new words. You can listen to the dialogue once more before giving your answers.

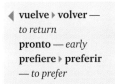

	correcto	falso
I. Agustín no tiene hambre.		
2. Agustín corta las patatas y las cebollas.		
3. Rosita siempre vuelve a casa muy pronto.		
4. Charo cree que Rosita tiene muchos amigos.		
5. A Charo Chema le parece buen chico.		
6. No hay vino para la cena.		
7. Agustín para beber prefiere vino.		
8. Agustín quiere comprar una botella de vino tinto y una cerveza.		

◀ **vuelve** ▶ **volver** —
to return
pronto — *early*
prefiere ▶ **preferir**
— *to prefer*

6

Listen to the dialogue on the CD while reading the text in the companion book. Underline the sentences in which someone is asked for a favor.

What do you say to indicate that you prefer something? Write the expression in the balloon.

To conclude, you can read the translation of the entire dialogue in the companion book.

*The verb **preferir** — The verb **traer***

7

§ 14 Irregular Verbs

The verb **preferir** (*to prefer*) is an irregular verb, with a change in the stem vowel (**e ▸ ie**). In the Grammar section, you will find all the conjugated forms of the verb.
Listen to the mini-dialogue on the CD. Play the second role and write down your answer. What do you prefer to drink? You can choose one of the drinks shown in the picture.

Hostess:	¿Qué prefieres para beber: agua o vino?
Guest:	_____
Hostess:	Yo tomo un agua.

8

Read the questions. Now listen to the four possible answers to each question on the CD, and choose whatever you prefer. You can mark more than one answer.

1. ¿Cómo prefiere cenar? a b c d

2. ¿Qué comida prefiere? a b c d

3. ¿Qué prefiere beber para cenar? a b c d

4. ¿Qué prefiere comprar en el mercado? a b c d

9

Try to fill in the blanks with the correct forms of the verb **traer** (*to bring; to carry*). Use the CD to check your answers.

traen — traemos — traes — traigo — trae — traéis

tú _____	Ana y tú _____	yo _____
Antonio _____	nosotras _____	ustedes _____

Note:
The verb **traer** is irregular in the first person singular (**yo**).

estar + *the present participle*

10

To describe an action that is in progress, use **estar** + the present participle:
¡Estoy preparando algo de cena! (*I'm preparing something for dinner!*)
The present participle is formed by adding an ending to the verb stem:
-ando for verbs ending in **-ar** and **-iendo** for verbs ending in **-er / -ir**. Listen
to the following three sentences on the CD, and write the missing forms of
estar + the present participle in the blanks.

> 1. La vecina _____ por teléfono.
>
> 2. Los niños _____ la televisión.
>
> 3. ¿Qué _____ ?

If the verb stem ends in a vowel, the ending **-endo** becomes **-yendo: leer** (*to
read*) ▸ **leyendo**
Other irregular present participles are:

ir ▸ yendo   decir ▸ diciendo   dormir ▸ durmiendo

▶ § 18 Present Participle

Good to know:
If the sentence con-
tains a pronoun, it ei-
ther precedes the verb
estar or is attached to
the end of the present
participle: **Le estoy
escribiendo una car-
ta. / Estoy escribién-
dole una carta.** In the
second case, a written
accent is required, to
retain the stress on
the same syllable of
the verb.

11

What are these people doing? Complete the sentences with the present
participle of the appropriate verb.

1. Agustín está   2. Jordi está   3. Rosita está   4. Charo está

_____   _____   _____   _____

en la oficina.   un plátano.   una novela.   la siesta.

12

Complete the sentences with the verbs provided, using a form of **estar** +
the present participle.

1. Las chicas (*patinar*) _____ .

2. ¿Qué (*beber*) _____ , Ana?

3. Rosita y yo (*comprar*) _____ el regalo para Noelia.

4. Rosita (*escribir*) _____ a sus padres.

5. Y vosotros, ¿también (*buscar*) _____ un piso en el centro?

*Adjectives vs. adverbs — **el mismo** / **la misma** / **lo mismo***

13

▶ § 9 Adverbs

▶ § 6 Adjectives

Good to know:

The use of the adverb **mal** (*badly*) and the adjectives **mal(o)**, **mala, malos, malas** (*bad*) resembles that of the adverb **bien** and the adjectives **buen(o), buena, buenos, buenas**. As an adjective, **malo** changes to **mal** (just as **bueno** changes to **buen**) when it precedes a noun: **No es un mal chico.**

Bien is an adverb; that is, it modifies verbs (**estar bien**), while **bueno / -a** is an adjective, and it gives additional information about (modifies) a noun or noun phrase (**Es una buena idea**).

In Spanish, adjectives usually <u>follow</u> the noun: **Un piso pequeño.** But sometimes they can <u>precede</u> the noun, for example, when a subjective assessment is being expressed: **Es una buena película.**

If the masculine form, **bueno**, <u>precedes</u> the noun, it is shortened to **buen:** **un buen vino; buena**, however, is never shortened.

Put the words in the correct blanks.

buen — bien — buen — bien

1. A ti Chema te cae muy _____ , ¿verdad?

3. Me parece _____ chico.

3. Se llevan muy _____ los dos.

4. ¿Puedes comprar un _____ vino tinto?

14

El mismo means *the same*, and as an adjective it agrees with the noun it modifies. Thus these forms exist: **El mismo / la misma / los mismos / las mismas** (*the same*), and they agree in number and gender with the noun they modify.

Complete the sentences with the appropriate form.

1. A Juan y a Carlos les gusta _____ chica.

2. ¿Sabes qué? Tú y yo tenemos _____ perfume.

3. A mis amigos y a mí nos gusta practicar _____ deportes.

4. Ese chico tiene _____ gafas que tú.

El mismo / la misma / los mismos / las mismas can also stand alone. In this case, there is an additional neutral form: **Lo mismo** (*the same*): **Noelia me ha comentado lo mismo.**

The use of the present perfect

15

As you already know, the present perfect is used to express actions and events that the speaker views as closely connected in time with the present. It often is used in connection with information such as **este año** (*this year*), **este mes** (*this month*), **esta semana** (*this week*), **hoy** (*today*), **todavía no** (*not yet*), **ya** (*already*).

The present perfect also is used in connection with statements of time such as **alguna vez** (*ever, in questions*), **muchas veces** (*many times*), **un par de veces** (*a couple of times*), **nunca** (*never*).

▶ § 15 Present Perfect

- **¿Has estado alguna vez en Latinoamérica?**
- **No, no he estado nunca, ¿y tú?**

Read the two questions and answer each. Use the expressions **nunca, una vez, un par de veces, muchas veces.**

¿Ya ha estado en España? (*Have you ever been in Spain?*)
¿Ha comido paella alguna vez? (*Have you ever eaten paella?*)

Good to know:

When **nunca** comes after the verb, a double negative is required:
<u>No</u> he estado <u>nunca</u> en Latinoamérica.
But if **nunca** precedes the verb, a double negative is not possible:
<u>Nunca</u> he estado en Latinoamérica.

16

Read the following sentences. Does this apply to you as well? If it does, answer **sí**, if not, answer **no**.

		sí	no
I.	He viajado muchas veces a Barcelona.		
2.	Todavía no he comido nada.		
3.	Este año he comprado un coche nuevo.		
4.	Ya he leído el periódico de hoy.		
5.	He estado un par de veces en México.		
6.	Nunca he practicado la vela.		
7.	He tenido que trabajar mucho esta semana.		
8.	He viajado una vez en el transiberiano.		

*The **tortilla***

17

Chema and Rosita are in the kitchen. Chema is showing her how to make a Spanish **tortilla.** First, read all the things you need to make a **tortilla.** Then listen to the dialogue several times, and try to put the pictures in the right order by numbering them from 1 to 6.

Ingredientes (*Ingredients*):
• 1 kg. de patatas
• 6 huevos (*eggs*)
• 1 cebolla pequeña
• ½ litro de aceite de oliva (*half a liter of olive oil*)
• 2 cucharaditas de sal (*teaspoons of salt*)

Otras cosas:
• una sartén para freír las patatas (*a pan for frying the potatoes*)
• un bol para batir los huevos (*a bowl for beating the eggs*)
• un plato para darle la vuelta a la tortilla (*a plate for turning the tortilla over*)

18

The **tortilla de patatas** — the popular omelet made of potatoes and eggs — is so typical a food in Spain that it is known, under the name **tortilla española**, as the national dish. The **tortilla** is often eaten for supper or as **tapas** in a bar.

In Spain today, a **tortilla** can be made with almost anything: With spinach or beans, with ham or mushrooms. In addition, there are many regional variations. For the simplest Madrid version, you fry the potatoes along with finely sliced onions or garlic cloves. Then the eggs are added to create an omelet. This **tortilla** is so popular that it is often thought to be the original recipe for the **tortilla de patatas** (though without onions).

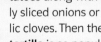

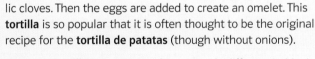

However, **tortilla** means something entirely different in Mexico, Central America, and the Caribbean. Here it refers to corn pancakes, made from cornmeal. In Mexico, they are filled with meat, for example, and called **enchiladas**.

Intercultural Tip

*Spanish **tapas** — Describing the day's events*

1 TR. 23

This is how a typical bar counter in Spain looks. Listen to the names of the various **tapas** (*tidbits, snacks*) on the CD and repeat them. Then look at the translations.

1. chopitos
2. callos
3. ensaladilla rusa
5. albóndigas
4. calamares a la romana
7. boquerones fritos
6. patatas bravas
10. aceitunas
8. jamón serrano
9. croquetas

*1. Deep-fried baby squid — 2. Tripe — 3. Russian salad —
4. Deep-fried squid — 5. Meatballs — 6. Spicy potatoes —
7. Deep-fried sardines — 8. Cured ham — 9. Croquettes — 10. Olives*

2 TR. 24 ✏

What is Agustín's day like? Look at the pictures and listen to the CD to hear how Agustín describes it. Then match the sentences below with the appropriate pictures. You will find information about the new vocabulary items on the right.

1.
2.
3.
4.
5.

a. Desayuno un café con leche y un cruasán. — b. Almuerzo con mis compañeros en la cantina. — c. Por las mañanas me levanto temprano. — d. Me acuesto siempre bastante tarde. — e. Termino de trabajar a las seis.

Good to know:
The verb forms **almuerzo** and **me acuesto** are the first person singular forms of the irregular verbs **almorzar** (*to eat lunch*) and **acostarse** (*to go to bed*).

◀ **me levanto** ▶
levantarse — *to rise, to get up*
temprano — *early*
desayunar — *to eat breakfast*
el cruasán — *croissant*
terminar — *to end, to finish*

noventa y nueve | 99

In their favorite bar

3

Chema and Jordi are in their favorite bar. They order some little snacks from Paco, the waiter, and talk about their different experiences at work that day.
Look at the picture and listen to the dialogue on the CD.

4

Listen to the following sentences from the dialogue on the CD, and read along. Can you match the English translations with the appropriate Spanish sentences? With a little intuition and imagination, you'll be sure to find the sentences that belong together.

1. ¿Nos pones una tapa de patatas bravas?

2. ¿Qué tal te van las prácticas en la empresa?

3. La ventaja es que termino antes.

4. Comer en tan poco tiempo es menos sano.

5. Comer no es tan importante como el tiempo libre.

6. En la empresa se empieza a trabajar a las ocho.

7. Yo prefiero comer con más tranquilidad.

8. Así puedo hacer deporte después del trabajo.

9. Veo que te levantas siempre muy temprano.

10. Se almuerza en la cantina.

a. *People eat in the canteen.*

b. *Eating is not as important as free time.*

c. *How is your internship in the company going?*

d. *This way I can play sports after work.*

e. *It's not so healthy to eat in such a short time.*

f. *The advantage is that I finish earlier.*

g. *I see that you always get up very early.*

h. *At the company, people start work at eight.*

i. *Can you bring us a **tapa** with **patatas bravas**?*

j. *I prefer eating with more peace and quiet.*

Talking about daily life

5

First, listen to the dialogue. Which of the following statements is made by Chema, and which by Jordi? Mark the correct answers. Then ask yourself whether these statements apply to you as well.

	Chema	Jordi	Usted
1. Está contento en su empresa.			
2. Se levanta siempre muy temprano para ir a trabajar.			
3. Tiene tiempo de desayunar y de leer el periódico por la mañana.			
4. Empieza a trabajar a las nueve de la mañana.			
5. A mediodía almuerza en un restaurante con los colegas.			
6. Le gusta comer con tranquilidad.			
7. Sale temprano del trabajo.			
8. Hace deporte después del trabajo.			

6

Listen to the entire dialogue once again while you read the text in the companion book. Can you tell from the dialogue what people say in Spanish to change the subject under discussion? Write the expression in the balloon.

Now you can underline any unfamiliar words and guess them from the context or look them up in the glossary.

*Reflexive verbs — The impersonal form **se***

7 👓

▶ § 21 Reflexive Verbs

The following sentences contain two reflexive verbs: **levantarse** (*to rise, get up*) and **acostarse** (*to go to bed*).
Te levantas siempre temprano. (*You always get up early.*)
Rosita se acuesta siempre muy tarde. (*Rosita always goes to bed very late.*)
You will find more information about reflexive verbs in the Grammar.

8 ✏

Fill in the blanks with the correct form of the verb in the present tense.

1. Jordi (*afeitarse*) _____ en diez minutos.

2. Yo siempre (*adaptarse*) _____ a todo rápidamente.

3. Creo que ustedes (*preocuparse*) _____ demasiado por ella.

4. Eva y yo (*encontrarse*) _____ muchas veces en la calle.

5. Sus amigos no (*atreverse*) _____ a decirle nada.

6. Vosotros dos (*llevarse*) _____ muy bien, ¿verdad?

9 👓 ✏

▶ § 22 Impersonal
Form **se**

En la empresa se empieza a trabajar a las ocho.
(*At the company, people start work at eight.*)
When people in general perform an action, the impersonal third person form **se** (*one, people, you*) is used in Spanish. The verb is in the third person singular.

Complete this sentence with the impersonal form **se**.

1. En el bar de Paco (*comer*) _____ un jamón muy bueno.

Now look at the following sentence:
En ese bar se comen (*one eats / you eat / people eat*) **unas croquetas muy ricas.**
If the grammatical subject of the Spanish sentence is a plural noun, the verb is also in the third person plural.

Complete these sentences with the impersonal **se**.

2. En el supermercado (*comprar*) _____ muchos productos.

3. En México (*hablar*) _____ español.

The impersonal form **se** *— Comparisons*

10 ✎

Use the impersonal **se** to complete these sentences about Spanish customs.

> ▶ § 22 **Impersonal Form se**

1. En España normalmente (*desayunar*) _____ poco.

2. (*almorzar*) _____ entre la una y las tres y media.

3. (*cenar*) _____ entre las nueve y las diez de la noche.

4. (*salir*) _____ mucho los fines de semana.

5. En los bares (*tomar*) _____ tapas y

   (*hablar*) _____ mucho.

6. (*tratar*) _____ a la gente de tú con mucha frecuencia.

7. No sólo (*bailar*) _____ flamenco.

11 👓

Para mí hacer deporte es <u>tan</u> importante <u>como</u> salir con los amigos. (*For me, playing sports is just as important as going out with friends.*) If you want to express equality in a comparison, use the following construction:

      tan + adjective (for example, **importante**) **+ como**
      just as + adjective (for example, *important*) *+ as*

If the object of the comparison is a noun, use **tanto / -a / -os / -as** instead of **tan**:

Chema tiene <u>tantos</u> amigos como Jordi.

> ▶ § 10 Comparisons

(*Chema has just as many friends as Jordi.*)

Note that **tanto / -a / -os / -as** has to agree in gender and number with the noun it modifies.

Fill in the blanks with the words given below.

> tan — tanto — tanta — tantas

1. Yo tengo _____ dinero como tú.

2. Aquí hay _____ comida como en un restaurante.

3. En esa empresa hay _____ secretarias como jefes.

4. Las patatas bravas están _____ ricas como los chopitos.

Comparisons

12

§ 10 Comparisons

You've just learned to make comparisons of equality. This equality can also be negated:
Comer en casa <u>no</u> es <u>tan</u> práctico <u>como</u> comer en la cantina.
(Eating at home is not as practical as eating in the canteen.)

This could also be expressed by a different comparison in which superiority is stated:
Comer en la cantina es <u>más</u> práctico <u>que</u> comer en casa.
(Eating in the canteen is more practical than eating at home.)

Or even by a comparison stating inferiority:
Comer en casa es <u>menos</u> práctico <u>que</u> comer en la cantina.
(Eating at home is less practical than eating in the canteen.)

Some adjectives do not form comparisons by using **más** or **menos**; they have their own, irregular comparative forms, such as:
bueno / -a (*good*) ▶ **mejor** (*better*)
malo / -a (*bad*) ▶ **peor** (*worse*)

Fill in the blanks by translating the words in parentheses into Spanish.

1. Yo trabajo (*more*) _____ horas (*than*) _____ tú.

2. Tú trabajas (*fewer*) _____ horas (*than*) _____ yo.

3. Tú no trabajas (*as many*) _____ horas (*as*) _____ yo.

13

Complete the sentences by translating the words provided into Spanish.

1. Nacho no es (*as shy as*) _____ Noelia.

2. Esta novela no es (*as good as*) _____ la otra.

3. Esos zapatos rojos son (*more extravagant than*) _____ éstos.

4. Tu jefa es (*nice than*) _____ mi secretaria.

5. Tienes (*as many plants as*) _____ mi vecina.

6. En esa tienda tienen (*as many sofas as*) _____ en la otra.

7. El autobús es (*more practical than*) _____ el coche.

8. Aquí hay (*fewer people than*) _____ en el bar de Paco.

The present participle — Expressing agreement and disagreement

14

You are already familiar with sentences containing **estar** + present participle (such as **estoy comiendo**). The present participle can also be used in connection with other verbs, such as **pasar** (*to spend, pass* [as time]).

▶ § 18 Present Participles

Listen to what Jordi has to say, and complete the sentence by filling in the missing words.

> Así puedo hacer un poco de deporte después del trabajo, salir con
>
> amigos o, si estoy muy estresado, pasar la tarde tranquilamente en
>
> casa _____ un libro o _____ la tele …

As the previous example shows, the present participle also can be used as a gerund to describe an action in progress. It refers to action that precedes or is simultaneous with the action of the other verb in the sentence. Sometimes it is translated into English by adding words such as "while" or "by":

Comiendo en la cantina se ahorra tiempo y dinero.
(*By eating in the canteen, you save time and money.*)

Good to know:

The present participle is also found in set phrases such as:
Oye Jordi, y hablando de otro tema, …
(*Tell me, Jordi, changing the subject, …*)

15

These sentences express agreement or contradiction:
Sí, tienes razón, aunque comer en tan poco tiempo es menos sano.
Sí, pero para mí comer mejor al mediodía no es tan importante como tener más tiempo libre.

Match the sentences on the left with the appropriate responses on the right. Use the CD to check your answers.

1. Hacer deporte es algo muy sano.	a. Sí, pero demasiado serio, ¿no crees?
2. Tu jefe me ha parecido muy amable.	b. No es verdad, era muy divertida.
3. Creo que no te ha gustado la película.	c. Estoy totalmente de acuerdo.

*Role play: A survey — Intercultural tip: **Tapas** bars*

16 TR. 29 🖉

Agustín is coming home from work and runs into an interviewer who is taking a survey. Listen to the dialogue. Then try to answer the questions by giving information about your own habits. Write down your responses.

Entrevistador: Perdone, señor. Estamos haciendo una encuesta sobre los horarios y las costumbres de los españoles. ¿Puede responder a un par de preguntas?

el entrevistador — ▶
interviewer
la encuesta —
survey
los horarios —
hours of work
las costumbres —
habits, customs
responder —
to answer
la pregunta —
question
por último — *as the last thing*

Usted: _____

Entrevistador: Muy bien. Usted, ¿a qué hora se levanta?

Usted: _____

Entrevistador: ¿Y a qué hora empieza a trabajar?

Usted: _____

Entrevistador: ¿Almuerza en su casa?

Usted: _____

Entrevistador: ¿Y a qué hora termina de trabajar?

Usted: _____

Entrevistador: ¿Lee el periódico todos los días?

Usted: _____

Entrevistador: Y ya por último, ¿a qué hora se acuesta usted?

Usted: _____

Entrevistador: Eso ha sido todo. Muchas gracias por su ayuda.

Usted: _____

17

There are bars everywhere in Spain—in cities as well as villages. The bar is a social meeting place where you can have a breakfast that includes coffee, **churros** (*thick, coiled fritters of fried dough*), or a **cruasán** (*croissant*). At midday, people go to the bar to have a snack, known as

tapas. At the end of the day people often have **tapas** again, usually with wine or beer. The bars usually are

quite crowded, and the atmosphere is relaxed and cheerful. There is loud talking, laughter, and a lot of smoking.

The bar, as a popular meeting place were people eat, drink, and chat in a casual atmosphere, is an important expression of the Spanish way of life, as is the custom of **tapas** bar hopping (**ir de tapeo**) in the evening.

Parts of the body — Describing physical complaints

1 TR. 30

Using the CD, listen to the terms for parts of the body and repeat them. The picture below will help you guess the meanings of the words!

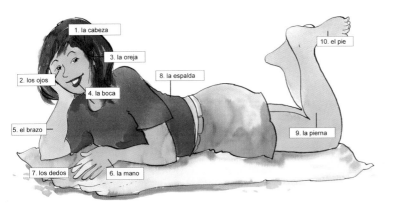

1. la cabeza
3. la oreja
10. el pie
8. la espalda
2. los ojos
4. la boca
5. el brazo
9. la pierna
7. los dedos
6. la mano

Good to know:

Be careful! Although it ends in **-o, mano** is a feminine noun: **la mano / las manos.**

2 TR. 31

Look at the people in the picture. **¿Qué les pasa?** (*What's wrong with them?*). Listen to the CD to find out what their problems are, and try to repeat the sentences. Then read the translations below.

1. Tengo fiebre.
2. Creo que tengo gripe.
3. Me siento mal.
4. Tengo dolor de cabeza.
5. Tengo tos.
6. Me duelen las piernas.
7. Tengo dolor de garganta.
8. Tengo dolor de muelas.
9. Estoy resfriado.
10. Me duele la espalda.

1. *I have a fever.* — 2. *I think I have the flu.* —
3. *I feel bad.* — 4. *I have a headache.* — 5. *I have a cough.*
6. *My legs hurt.* — 7. *I have a sore throat.* —
8. *I have a toothache.* — 9. *I have a bad cold.* — 10. *My back hurts.*

In the family doctor's waiting room

3

Noelia and Rosita meet by chance in the waiting room of the family doctor. They talk about their complaints and … about men! Look at the pictures and listen to the dialogue several times.

4

Listen to some sentences from the dialogue on the CD and repeat them. Then read the translations.

1. ¡Qué casualidad!	a. *What a coincidence!*
2. ¿Qué te pasa?	b. *What's wrong with you?*
3. ¡Vaya!	c. *What a pity!*
4. Parecen síntomas de estrés …	d. *They seem to be symptoms of stress …*
5. Eso no es sano.	e. *That's not healthy.*
6. Es importante descansar …	f. *It's important to rest …*
7. ¿A qué te refieres?	g. *What do you mean?*
8. Chema no es mi tipo.	h. *Chema is not my type.*
9. ¡Jordi es demasiado delgado!	i. *Jordi is too thin!*
10. ¡Que te mejores!	j. *I hope you feel better soon!*

Wishing someone a speedy recovery — Giving advice

5 TR. 32

Listen to the dialogue several times. Then mark these statements as true or false.

> **Good to know:**
> In the verb **dormir** (*to sleep*), the stem vowel changes from **o** to **ue** in the forms that are stressed on the stem vowel: **Rosita duerme poco.**

		correcto	falso
1.	Noelia está resfriada pero no tiene fiebre.		
2.	Rosita tiene dolor de espalda y se siente cansada.		
3.	Noelia cree que Rosita tiene estrés.		
4.	Rosita trabaja mucho y duerme siete horas al día.		
5.	Noelia le dice a Rosita que tiene que dormir más.		
6.	A Rosita le gusta Chema.		
7.	Noelia opina que Jordi es demasiado delgado.		
8.	Rosita está contenta con sus compañeros de piso.		

6 TR. 32

Listen to the dialogue again as you read the text in the companion book. How does Noelia say that she hopes Rosita will feel better soon? Write the expression in the balloon.

Noelia gives Rosita several pieces of advice. Find these places in the text and underline them.

7 TR. 34

Listen to the following pieces of advice and repeat them.

> Hay que tomar mucha vitamina C.
> *You have to take a lot of vitamin C.*
>
> Para relajarse es muy bueno hacer yoga.
> *To relax, it's really good to do yoga.*
>
> Un jarabe hace bien contra el dolor de garganta.
> *A syrup is good for a sore throat.*

> **Good to know:**
> Please note: *something for the pain* can be expressed in Spanish with **algo <u>contra</u>** as well as **algo <u>para</u> el dolor.**

*The verbs **doler** and **sentirse** — Adverbs*

8

▶ **§ 14 Irregular Verbs**

The verb **doler** (*to hurt*) is irregular, because the stem vowel **o** changes to **ue** in the forms that are stressed on the stem vowel:

> **Me d<u>ue</u>len las piernas.** (*My legs hurt.*)

Translate the following sentence.

> Do your feet hurt? _____

Good to know:

In Spanish, the possessive is not used in such constructions. You need to say: **Me duele la cabeza.**

The reflexive verb **sentirse** (*to feel*) is also an irregular verb, in which the stem vowel **e** changes to **ie** in the forms that are stressed on the stem:

> **Me s<u>ie</u>nto muy cansada.** (*I feel very tired.*)

Use the verb **sentirse** to complete the following sentences.

1. ¿Cómo _____ , mamá?

2. Nosotros _____ muy bien aquí.

3. Las chicas _____ un poco mal.

9

▶ **§ 9 Adverbs**

Adverbs can be derived from adjectives by attaching the ending **-mente** to the feminine form of the adjective:

> **seguro / -a** (*certain*) ▶ **seguramente** (*certainly*)

Good to know:

Watch out: If the adjective has a written accent, the adverb does too (for example, **fácilmente**).

If the adjective has only one form for masculine and feminine, the ending **-mente** is directly attached to it:

> **fácil** (*easy*) ▶ **fácilmente** (*easily*)

Form the adverb corresponding to each of the following adjectives.

1. amable — 2. estupendo — 3. normal — 4. sincero

10

▶ **§ 9 Adverbs**

Complete the sentences with the appropriate adverbs.

1. Hemos ido (*directo/a*) _____ al hospital.

2. ¿Por qué no se lo dices (*personal*) _____ ?

3. Te ha mirado muy (*serio/a*) _____ .

4. Me ha dicho (*tímido/a*) _____ que sí.

5. Tienes que volver a casa (*rápido/a*) _____ .

*Impersonal expressions — The expression **hay que***

11

Impersonal expressions can be formed by using the construction **(no) es** + adjective + infinitive:

> §23 Infinitive
> Constructions

<u>Es importante</u> descansar. *(It is important to rest.)*
<u>No es fácil</u> encontrar compañeros de piso tan agradables.
(It is not easy to find such pleasant apartment mates.)

2
TR. 35

Listen to the following sentences on the CD and fill in the missing impersonal expressions.

1. _____ compartir piso con amigos.

2. _____ tener siempre dolor de cabeza.

3. _____ dormir tan poco.

12

You are already familiar with the expression **tener que** + infinitive as a way to state an obligation or necessity, as in these examples:

> **Tengo que trabajar.** *(I have to work.)*

This can also be expressed impersonally, with **hay que**:

> **Hay que trabajar.** *(It is necessary to work.)*

This is how Noelia formulates her advice to Rosita:

> **Hay que dormir siete horas como mínimo.**
> *(It is necessary to sleep a minimum of seven hours.)*

2
TR. 36   Listen to the following three suggestions for leading a healthy life.

Hay que comer con tranquilidad.

Hay que hacer deporte.

¡Hay que sonreír!

Stressed possessives — Describing people

13 👓 ✏️

▶ § 34 Possessives

Pero tu <u>familia</u> está cerca, ¡y <u>la mía</u> está tan lejos!
(But your family is nearby, and mine is so far away!)
The stressed possessives (with definite article) are used to avoid repeating previously mentioned nouns.
Here you see all the forms of the stressed possessives:

Good to know:

If you ask who the owner is, no article is used before the possessive:
- **¿Son tuyas estas flores?** (*Are these your flowers? or Are these flowers yours?*)
- **Sí, son mías.** (*Yes, they are mine.*)

mío, mía / míos, mías	**nuestro, nuestra / nuestros, nuestras**
tuyo, tuya / tuyos, tuyas	**vuestro, vuestra / vuestros, vuestras**
suyo, suya / suyos, suyas	**suyo, suya / suyos, suyas**

Translate the possessives given below into Spanish.

1. • Mis hijos van al cine con mucha frecuencia.

   ○ (*mine*) _____ , también, pero (*hers*) _____ , prefieren ver la tele.

2. • Su hermana es enfermera.

   ○ (*ours*) _____ también; y (*yours,* fam. sing.) _____ , ¿qué hace?

14 🔊 2 TR.37 ✏️

Listen to the following descriptions of people on the CD and repeat them. Then try to match the translations below with the corresponding Spanish sentences.

Good to know:

The verbs **ser** and **tener** are used to express lasting states or conditions: **Es alta, tiene el pelo liso.** For temporary or accidental states, the verb **llevar** (*to wear; to carry*) is used: **Lleva el pelo corto.**

9 Es joven.   3 Tiene el pelo rubio.   4 Tiene el pelo corto.
5 Tiene el pelo rizado.
10 No es alta ni baja.   1 Lleva barba.
2 Tiene los ojos castaños.   7 Es moreno.
6 Tiene el pelo liso.
8 Es un hombre mayor.

■ a. *He has short hair.* — ■ b. *He is young.* — ■ c. *He has blond hair.*
■ d. *He is an older man.* — ■ e. *She has curly hair.* —
■ f. *He has a beard.* — ■ g. *He is dark-haired.* —
■ h. *She has straight hair.* — ■ i. *She is neither tall nor short.* —
■ j. *She has brown eyes.*

Describing people — Expressing wishes

15

Listen to the descriptions of our friends. Match the numbers of the sentences with the persons they describe in the picture below.

1. Es una chica delgada, morena, de ojos negros y tiene el pelo bastante largo.
2. Es bastante alto y muy delgado; es moreno, de ojos negros y tiene el pelo corto.
3. Tiene los ojos castaños y el pelo negro. No lleva barba ni bigote.
4. Es joven: sólo tiene 20 años. Es delgada y tiene el pelo corto y liso.
5. Tiene los ojos castaños. Tiene el pelo castaño y lo lleva un poco largo. También lleva barba.
6. Es una señora mayor; es bajita y tiene el pelo blanco.
7. No es alta ni baja. Tiene los ojos castaños y lleva el pelo corto.

16

A mí también <u>me gustaría</u> ser independiente y compartir piso con amigos.
(I too would like to be independent and share an apartment with friends.)
To express a wish you can use the expression **me / te / . . . gusta** in the conditional mood, that is, **me / te / . . . gustaría**.

Give personal answers to the following two questions. You can listen to some possible answers on the CD.

¿Adónde le gustaría ir este fin de semana?
¿Dónde le gustaría tener una casa?

A song — A crossword puzzle

17

el burro — *donkey* ▶	Listen to the song titled **A mi burro** on the CD. Because it is a children's song, it contains many diminutives ending in **-ito / -ita**. Put the pictures in the order in which the scenes appear in the song, and number them from 1 to 6.
la gorrita — *small cap*	
los zapatitos — *small shoes*	
lila — *lilac*	
tieso/a — *stiff*	
el corazón — *heart*	
el limón — *lemon*	
la pezuña — *hoof*	

18

Read the definitions and write the appropriate words in the crossword puzzle.

1. ¡Una parte del cuerpo muy importante!
2. Si usted tiene fiebre y se siente muy cansado tiene síntomas de…
3. Algo para el dolor de cabeza.
4. Una parte del cuerpo que sirve para hablar.
5. Algo para el dolor de garganta.
6. Una parte del cuerpo que sirve para caminar.
7. Algo que se toma para estar sano.

Dishes — The preterit

1 TR. 41

The names of some dishes are missing from this menu. Listen to them on the CD, and then try to write the words in the correct boxes. Then read the translations of the dishes below.

◀ **el menú** — *menu*
el primer plato — *first course*
el segundo plato — *second course*
el postre — *dessert*
incluido — *included*

CASA PANCHO
Menú del día

Primo plato:

Segundo plato:

Postre:

yogur

vino, agua y

12,50 EUR
(iVA incluido)

sopa de pescado

pollo asado con patatas

chuletas de cordero a la brasa

ensalada mixta — gazpacho — pulpo a la gallega — merluza a la romana — bacalao al pil pil — flan — fruta del tiempo — helado — pan

Good to know:

The Spanish **I.V.A. (impuesto sobre el valor añadido)** is the value added tax, or VAT. Normally it is included in the price; if not, that fact is specially noted.

el bacalao al pil pil — *cod with chili peppers and garlic*
la chuleta de cordero a la brasa — *grilled lamb chop*
la ensalada mixta — *mixed salad*
el flan — *crème caramel*
la fruta del tiempo — *fresh fruit in season*
el gazpacho — *chilled soup with chopped vegetables*

el helado — *ice cream*
la merluza a la romana — *hake fried in batter*
el pollo asado — *roast chicken*
el pulpo a la gallega — *octopus Galician style*
la sopa de pescado — *fish soup*
el yogur — *yogurt*

2 TR. 42

On the CD, listen to what these people did yesterday (**ayer**) or recently (**el otro día**). The words given are the verb forms used.

◀ **ayudó** (▶ **ayudar**) — *he / she/ it helped*
compré (▶ **comprar**) — *I bought*
dijo (▶ **decir**) — *he / she / it said*
hicimos (▶ **hacer**) — *we made*

ayudó · compré · dijo · hicimos

Noelia's birthday

3

It's Noelia's birthday, and Chema invites her to dinner in a restaurant. Look at the pictures and listen to the dialogue several times.

4

Listen to the conversation between Chema and Noelia several times, and then mark the sentences that fit the dialogue.

1. ■ Noelia pide de primer plato bacalao al pil pil.
2. ■ Chema quiere tomar chuletas de cordero.
3. ■ Noelia quiere beber vino tinto y agua.
4. ■ El camarero le trae a Noelia un vino del Penedés.
5. ■ Chema y Rosita no se llevan muy bien.
6. ■ Noelia cree que a Chema le gusta Rosita.
7. ■ Chema le regala a Noelia un casco.
8. ■ A Noelia le encanta el regalo de Chema.

5

Now listen to the dialogue again while reading the text in the companion book. What did Chema and Rosita do together? Underline these parts of the text.
How do you say "Congratulations!" in Spanish? Write the expression in the balloon.

Congratulations!

Birthday songs — A set table — Foods

6

Listen to three Spanish birthday songs on the CD and fill in the blanks below with the missing lyrics.

1. ¡_____ feliz!, ¡cumpleaños feliz!

     te _____ todos, ¡cumpleaños feliz!

2. Es un muchacho _____ (*3 veces*)

     y _____ lo será, y siempre lo será.

3. Feliz, feliz en tu _____, amiguita que Dios te bendiga

     que reine la paz en tu día, ¡y que _____ muchos más!

◀ **¡Feliz cumpleaños!**
— *Happy Birthday!*
excelente —
excellent, great
siempre lo será
— *he will always
be that*
**que Dios te bendi-
ga** — *God bless you*
que reine la paz
— *may peace reign*
**¡Que cumplas mu-
chos más!** — *May
you have many more*

7

Here you see a table that has been set. Listen to the words and repeat them.

10. el aceite y el vinagre
8. el vaso
1. el mantel
7. la cucharilla
9. la sal
2. la servilleta
3. el plato
6. la cuchara
4. el tenedor
5. el cuchillo

Good to know:
Certain styles of preparation are common in Spanish cuisine: **Al ajillo** (*with garlic*), **a la romana** (*fried in batter*), **a la plancha** (*grilled*), **al horno** (*oven-baked*), **asado** (*roasted*), **cocido** (*boiled*), **frito** (*deep-fat fried*).

8

Listen to the names of the following foods and repeat them. Then write out a menu and place the foods in these categories: Appetizers (**Entradas**), Meat and Fish (**Carne y pescado**), and Desserts (**Postres**).

Almejas a la marinera — *Clams in tomato sauce*
Arroz con leche — *Rice pudding*
Consomé de pollo — *Chicken consommé*
Cordero asado con patatas — *Roast lamb with potatoes*
Crema catalana — *Catalan custard*
Crema de espárragos — *Cream of asparagus*
Escalope de ternera — *Veal cutlet*
Merluza a la cazuela — *Hake in an earthenware casserole*

Good to know:
Don't forget: To talk about food, use the verb **estar: Este gazpacho está muy rico.**

Interrogatives — Relative clauses

9

§ 36 Interrogatives

The interrogative **¿cuál?** (pl.: **¿cuáles?**) means *which (one)? what?*:
Me gustaría tomar un vino blanco. ¿Cuál me recomienda?
(I'd like to drink a white wine. Which one can you recommend to me?)
The interrogative **¿qué?** can also mean *which? what?*, but it always accompanies a noun and is invariable:
¿Qué vino me recomienda? (*Which wine can you recommend to me?*)

TR. 47

Fill in the blanks with the correct interrogatives, and use the CD to check your answers.

1. De estos platos, ¿ _____ no te gustan?   cuál

2. ¿ _____ es tu plato favorito?   qué

3. A ti, ¿ _____ postre te gusta más?   cuáles

10

Complete these mini-dialogues by using **cuál, cuáles,** or **qué**.

1. • ¿ _____ número de teléfono tienes?

   ○ ¿ _____ quieres: el número de casa o el de la oficina?

2. • Mira, éstos son mis primos.

   ○ ¿ _____ ?, ¿los de Madrid?

3. • ¿ _____ libros has comprado?

   ○ He comprado los libros que me dijiste.

11

§ 35 Relative Pronouns

Good to know:

As you can see from the exercise, the relative pronoun **que** is used for masculine and feminine nouns, in both singular and plural, and as object or subject.

The waiter in the dialogue says to Noelia:
Tenemos un vino del Penedés <u>que está muy bueno</u>.
(We have a wine from the Penedés region that is very good.)
The underlined clause is a so-called relative clause, which gives more information about **vino**. The relative pronoun **que** (*that; which; who; whom*) connects the two sentences here: **Tenemos un vino. + El vino está muy bueno.**

Please link the following sentences.

1. Rosita es una chica. Ella siempre está dispuesta a ayudar.
2. Chema y Rosita son dos compañeros de piso. Ellos se llevan muy bien.

The preterit (indefinido)

12 TR. 48

The dialogue for this lesson presents a past tense form, the preterit (in Spanish, indefinido), that is new to you. Listen to two sentences on the CD that contain the missing verb forms, and use them to complete the conjugation of the **-ar** verbs below.

> ▶ § 16 Preterit
> (Indefinido)

yo	habl-**é**,	nosotros/as	aprovech-_____
tú	cont-**aste**	vosotros/as	compr-**asteis**
él, ella, usted	coment-_____	ellos/as, ustedes	ayud-**aron**

Verbs ending in **-er** and **–ir** follow the same conjugational pattern in the preterit:

yo	com-**í**/viv-**í**
tú	com-**iste**/viv-**iste**
él, ella, usted	com-**ió**/viv-**ió**
nosotros, nosotras	com-**imos**/viv-**imos**
vosotros, vosotras	com-**isteis**/viv-**isteis**
ellos, ellas, ustedes	com-**ieron**/viv-**ieron**

Good to know:

In verbs ending in –ar and –ir, the first person plural forms are identical (-**amos**, -**imos**) to the present tense forms. But the context always makes it clear which tense is intended.

13

The forms of **ser** and **ir** in the preterit are identical and regular. You can tell from the context which verb is intended:

Yo fui a su casa ayer. *(I went to his / her house yesterday.)*
El otro día no fuiste muy amable con tu abuela.
(You weren't very nice to your grandmother the other day.)
Ustedes fueron ayer al teatro, ¿verdad?
(You went to the theater yesterday, didn't you?)

> ▶ § 16 Preterit
> (Indefinido)

  TR. 49

Put the verb forms below in the correct blanks, and use the CD to check your answers.

> fuisteis — fue — fuimos

Rosita _____ una ayuda fantástica.

Rosita y yo _____ a buscar un regalo para una amiga.

Rosita y tú _____ juntos de compras, ¿verdad?

Good to know:

Some important verbs have an irregular stem in the preterit, including **hacer ▶ hic-** and **decir ▶ dij-**.

The preterit (indefinido)

14

▶ § 16 Preterit
(Indefinido)

The verbs **tener** and **estar** have irregular stems in the preterit: **Tener ▶ tuv-**, **estar ▶ estuv-**. Look at the forms of **tener** below.

yo	**tuv**-e	nosotros, nosotras	**tuv**-imos
tú	**tuv**-iste	vosotros, vosotras	**tuv**-isteis
él, ella, usted	**tuv**-o	ellos, ellas, ustedes	**tuv**-ieron

Fill in the blanks with the correct forms of **estar**, and use the CD to check your answers.

> estuvieron — estuvo — estuvimos — estuviste — estuve — estuvisteis

1. Rosita _____ aquí el otro día.

2. Los chicos _____ el otro día en un centro comercial.

3. Ayer Agustín y yo _____ en casa de unos amigos;

   y vosotros, ¿dónde _____ ?

4. Ayer _____ en el nuevo museo de arte. Y tú, Chema,

   ¿dónde _____ ?

15

Complete the following sentences, using the appropriate preterit form of the verbs given.

1. El otro día (*nosotros/cenar*) _____ en el restaurante Casa Pancho.

2. ¿Dónde (*estar*) _____ ayer, Rosita?

3. Mi abuelo (*viajar*) _____ a Cuba en el año 1930.

4. Y vosotras, ¿por qué no (*ir*) _____ a la fiesta de cumpleaños?

5. ¿Qué te (*decir*) _____ ayer los compañeros?

6. La abuela (*ver*) _____ ayer la última película de Almodóvar.

7. ¿Qué (*hacer*) _____ ustedes la semana pasada?

8. Vosotras no me (*decir*) _____ eso.

9. Ellos (*conocerse*) _____ el año pasado.

10. El otro día (*yo/tener*) _____ que hablar seriamente con él.

The use of the preterit

16

The preterit is used to talk about completed past events that occurred at a certain time or in a certain space of time and have no reference to the moment of speaking. Therefore, the preterit often appears in connection with the following expressions of time: **El otro día** (*the other* day), **ayer** (*yesterday*), **la semana pasada** (*last week*), **el mes pasado** (*last month*), **el año pasado** (*last year*), **en 1970** (*in 1970*).

▶ § 16 Preterit
(Indefinido)

Good to know:
The preterit is used instead of the present perfect in some regions of Spain and in most Latin American countries: **¿Adónde fuiste hoy?** Instead of **¿Adónde has ido hoy?**

Listen to the following sentences, and put the time expressions in the correct blanks.

> el otro día — ayer — el año pasado — el sábado por la noche

1. Mi familia y yo estuvimos en Sevilla _____ .

2. ¿No fuiste al cine _____ ?

3. _____ vi a doña Amparo paseando con sus amigas.

4. _____ no cenaron en casa; fueron al restaurante de Pancho.

17 TR. 52

Listen to the dialogue between Rosita and a girlfriend, and put the pictures in chronological order by numbering them from 1 to 6.

Role play: At a restaurant — Intercultural tip: At a restaurant in Spain

18 🖎

Today Agustín is in Barcelona on a business trip, and he's eating in a restaurant. Listen to the dialogue between Agustín and the waiter. Play the role of Agustín and order what you would like to eat.

Camarero: ¡Buenas tardes, señor!
You return his greeting and ask what the daily specials are:
_____

Camarero: Pues de primero tenemos crema de espárragos, gazpacho y ensalada mixta y, de segundo, cordero asado con patatas, merluza a la cazuela y escalope de ternera.
You order whatever you would like:
_____

Camarero: Muy bien. ¿Y para beber?
You order something to drink: _____
Camarero: Enseguida.
*You say thank you:*_____
- — -
Camarero: ¿Qué tal la merluza?
*You say whether you like it:*_____
Camarero: ¿Desea tomar algo de postre? Hay fruta del tiempo, helado, flan, yogur, queso, arroz con leche, …
You order a dessert: _____
Camarero: Muy bien.
- — -
Camarero: ¿Desea algo más?
You order coffee and ask for the check:
_____

19

Eating and going out to eat have a special social and communicative function in Spain. Even business is discussed over dinner. All this lends restaurants an especially lively atmosphere. Usually one person pays the check for everyone in the group, but among young people sometimes each one pays separately.

When you leave the tip (**la propina**), just round up the amount, as a service charge is already included. Only if the service was especially obliging should you possibly give a larger tip than usual. After you pay, leave the tip on the little dish on which the waiter usually brings your change. Otherwise, just leave it on the table.

Reacting properly

1

Match the Spanish sentences on the right with the corresponding para-phrases on the left.

1. *talking about food*	a. ¿Puedes ayudarme en la cocina?
2. *congratulating someone*	b. Este regalo es para ti.
3. *presenting a gift*	c. Tienes que beber más agua.
4. *giving advice*	d. ¡Muchas felicidades, hija!
5. *asking a favor*	e. La paella está muy rica.

2 TR. 54

Match the sentences on the left with the appropriate reactions on the right, and use the CD to check your answers.

1. ¿Qué te gustaría hacer el día de tu cumpleaños?	a. La verdad es que todavía no lo he pensado.
2. ¿Qué hicisteis el domingo pasado?	b. ¿Tienen crema catalana?
3. ¿Adónde preferís ir los sábados por la noche?	c. Pero, ¿por qué os habéis molestado?
4. Os hemos traído algo de Salamanca.	d. Estuvimos cenando en casa de unos amigos.
5. ¿Desea tomar alguna cosa de postre?	e. Yo al cine, pero a mi mujer le gusta más ir a bailar.

Answering questions — Describing someone's appearance

3

Read the questions and mark the answer or answers that apply to you.

1. ¿Qué hace después del trabajo?
   - a. ■ Me gusta leer el periódico/un libro.
   - b. ■ Veo la televisión.
   - c. ■ Hago deporte.
   - d. ■ Salgo con los amigos.

2. ¿Cómo se siente hoy?
   - a. ■ ¡Estupendamente!
   - b. ■ Bastante bien.
   - c. ■ No muy bien.
   - d. ■ Mal.

3. ¿A qué país le gustaría viajar?
   - a. ■ A Perú.
   - b. ■ A México.
   - c. ■ A Chile.
   - d. ■ A Cuba.

4

Fill in the blanks with the correct verbs.

> tiene — lleva — es

Ella _____ morena, _____ los ojos negros y _____ gafas.

Do you remember how to describe someone's appearance?
The verbs **ser** and **tener** are used for permanent and characteristic features: **Es rubio** (*he is blond*), **tiene los ojos azules** (*he / she has blue eyes*). For temporary and impermanent characteristics, use the verb **llevar: Lleva bigote** (*he has a mustache*), **lleva el pelo corto** (*he / she wears his / her hair short*).

Now listen to the dialogue between Chema and Jordi, in which they talk about the appearance of a girl Jordi knows. And you, how do you look? Describe your appearance. You can listen to the dialogue several times if you need help. Suggested answers are given in the companion book.

The present participle — Relative clauses

5

Do you remember the construction **estar** + present participle? If not, review the appropriate chapter in the Grammar.

▶ § 18 Present Participles

Complete the following sentences by filling in the blanks with the appropriate form of **estar** + present participle.

1. Los chicos (*estudiar*) _____ en la biblioteca.

2. ¿Qué (*beber*) _____ ustedes?

3. Y vosotras, ¿dónde (*vivir*) _____ ahora?

4. Perdone, ¿(*esperar*) _____ usted al autobús?

5. Rosita y yo (*hacer*) _____ una tortilla.

6. ¿(*leer*) _____ este libro, Jordi?

7. Yo no te (*decir*) _____ eso.

8. La abuela (*dormir*) _____ la siesta.

6

What are these people doing? Look at the pictures, and complete the sentences with the proper form of **estar** + present participle.

1. Agustín _____ con unos colegas en la cantina.

2. Las chicas _____ de sus problemas de salud.

3. Noelia y Chema _____ en un restaurante.

7

Connect the following sentences by using the relative pronoun **que**.

▶ § 35 Relative Pronouns

1. Salamanca es una ciudad. La ciudad de Salamanca me gusta.

2. Rosita tiene muchos amigos. Sus amigos trabajan en el museo.

Comparisons — The impersonal form **se** *— Adverb vs. adjective*

8

▶ § 10 Comparisons

Good to know:
Please make a note of these irregular comparatives:
mejor (◀ **bueno / -a**)
peor (◀ **malo / -a**)

Do you remember how to make comparisons in Spanish? If you're no longer sure, look at the Grammar section.

What word is missing in these sentences? Write the words in the correct blanks.

> tanto — tan — mejor — más — tantos — como — tantas — más

1. Chema tiene _____ trabajo como Jordi.

2. Ese restaurante es _____ caro como Casa Pancho.

3. Rosita se siente hoy _____ que ayer.

4. Agustín trabaja _____ horas que su secretaria.

5. El cordero está _____ rico que el pollo asado.

6. Ella tiene _____ problemas como tú.

7. Tu coche no es tan rápido _____ el mío.

8. Aquí hay _____ tapas como en el bar de Paco.

9

▶ § 22 Impersonal
Form **se**

Rewrite the following sentences, using the impersonal **se.**

1. En este restaurante comes muy bien por muy poco dinero.

2. En Madrid puedes hacer muchas cosas interesantes.

10

▶ § 6 Adjectives

▶ § 9 Adverbs

Complete the following sentences by adding the adverb **bien** or the adjective **buen(o) / -a / -os / -as**.

1. Casa Pancho es un _____ restaurante.

2. ¿Os lleváis _____ con el jefe?

3. Noelia es una _____ estudiante.

4. No me parece _____ eso que estás haciendo.

5. Los vinos de aquí son muy _____ .

Verbs in the present, present perfect, and preterit — Present perfect vs. preterit

11 ✎

Each form in these three tables has to be entered in the other two tenses. For example, if you see **soy** on the first line, then you have to enter in the other two columns. Remember that each line refers to a specific person (*first, second, …*).

▶ § 14 Irregular Verbs

▶ § 15 Present Perfect

▶ § 16 Preterit (Indefinido)

Present	Present Perfect	Preterit
soy		
	has tenido	
		hizo
estamos		
	habéis ido	
		dijeron

12 👓 ✎

Review the difference between the present perfect and the preterit:

The present perfect is used to express actions and events that the speaker sees as closely related to the moment of speaking.

▶ § 15 Present Perfect

▶ § 16 Preterit (Indefinido)

The preterit is used to express actions and events that have no reference to the moment of speaking.

Complete the following sentences by putting the verbs given in the appropriate tense (present perfect or preterit) and writing them in the blanks.

1. El año pasado Jordi (*hacer*) _____ unas prácticas en Barcelona.

2. Rosita y yo no (*poder*) _____ ir esta semana a la piscina.

3. Rosita (*ir*) _____ al médico la semana pasada.

4. ¿Tú (*estar*) _____ alguna vez en Salamanca?

5. Yo sólo la (*ver*) _____ un par de veces.

6. Noelia y Chema (*cenar*) _____ el otro día en un restaurante.

7. Yo no (*hablar*) _____ con ella todavía.

8. Nosotros lo (*conocer*) _____ en Barcelona en 1995.

Foods and drinks — Setting the table

13

What's all this? In the strings of letters, try to find the term that matches
the paraphrase, and mark it.

1. Algo que puede ser de naranja, de manzana, de plátano, … :

   botrefreszumocomostelevino

2. Un postre que puede ser de chocolate, de fresa, de nata, … :

   flaramelgurotagurheladotaso

3. Algo muy español que hay en muchos bares:

   canapisalbonditortillamatisol

4. Algo que se toma como tapa:

   quesimanaceitunasoranpanos

5. Una sopa fría:

   pescadigazpachogallecalgoto

14

You need these objects in order to set the table. What are they called in
Spanish?

8.

7.

6.

1.

2.

3.

4.

5.

Parts of the body — A postcard from Salamanca

15 ✎

Match the parts of the body shown on the left with the correct words on the right.

1.

2.

3.

a. los ojos

b. la mano

c. la espalda

16 ✎

Read these questions and mark the correct answer.

1. What is **la propina**?
   a. ■ The check.
   b. ■ The change.
   c. ■ The tip.

2. Mexican **tortillas** are
   a. ■ made from cornmeal.
   b. ■ made from potatoes.
   c. ■ made from potatoes and eggs.

17 ✎

Fill in the blanks in this postcard that Rosita is writing to her girlfriend.

¡Hola, Juanita!

¿Cómo estás? Ya _____ he adaptado a todo aquí: a la ciudad, al trabajo, al piso, … ¡y a la comida española!

En España _____ desayuna muy _____ . Yo ahora tomo sólo un café y un cruasán; a _____ , incluso, no desayuno nada.

La semana pasada _____ en Salamanca, la ciudad _____ te gusta tanto. _____ con unos amigos y nos divertimos mucho.

Hoy no he ido al museo porque no me _____ bien. El _____ me ha dicho que tengo que trabajar _____ .

Un saludo, Rosita

Elision — Describing the day's activities

18

In Spanish, sounds are omitted as words are combined into phrases and sentences. This omission, or elision, is especially common when a word ends in a vowel and the next one also begins with a vowel:

2
TR. 56   Listen to the following sentences, paying attention to the way some words are run together. Repeat the sentences.

> Por las mañanas se levanta pronto para ir al museo y se acuesta siempre muy tarde.
>
> Traigo una botella de tinto y una de cerveza, ¿vale?
>
> El otro día os vi a los dos en el Centro Comercial San Isidro.

When two or three identical vowels follow one another, they are spoken as one, though a bit longer:

2
TR. 57   Listen to the following two sentences and repeat them.

> Ella me dijo otra cosa.
>
> Siempre está dispuesta a ayudar.

19

These pictures are out of order. On the CD, listen to the young man telling how he has spent the day, and put the pictures in the correct chronological order by numbering them from 1 to 6.

The weather — Describing feelings and moods

1 TR. 59

What's the weather like in Latin America? Listen to the expressions on the CD. Can you guess their meanings with the help of the picture? Compare your guesses with the translations below.

Good to know:

Keep in mind: Many weather-related expressions use the verb **hacer: hace buen / mal tiempo, hace sol / calor / frío / viento.**

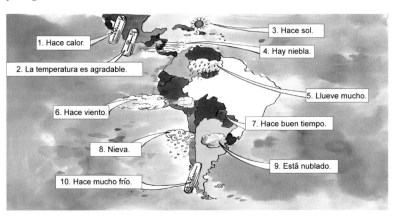

1. Hace calor.
2. La temperatura es agradable.
3. Hace sol.
4. Hay niebla.
5. Llueve mucho.
6. Hace viento.
7. Hace buen tiempo.
8. Nieva.
9. Está nublado.
10. Hace mucho frío.

1. *It's hot.* — 2. *The temperature is pleasant.* — 3. *It's sunny.* —
4. *It's foggy.* — 5. *It rains a lot.* — 6. *It's windy.* — 7. *The weather is good.* —
8. *It's snowing.* — 9. *It's cloudy.* — 10. *It's very cold.*

2 TR. 60

Listen to the CD to find out about these people's feelings and moods. Then match the expressions with the appropriate pictures. You will find the translations in the vocabulary box on the right.

Good to know:

To express temporary feelings and states of mind, the verb **estar** is used: **estar bien / nervioso / cansado.**

1.  2.   3.   4.

5.   6.   7.

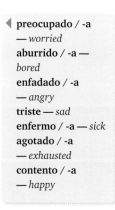

preocupado / -a — *worried*
aburrido / -a — *bored*
enfadado / -a — *angry*
triste — *sad*
enfermo / -a — *sick*
agotado / -a — *exhausted*
contento / -a — *happy*

a. Está contenta. — b. Está preocupada. — c. Está enfadado. —
d. Está enfermo. — e. Está aburrido. — f. Está triste. — g. Está agotada.

Noelia comes home

3

After having dinner with Chema, Noelia doesn't get home until late in the evening. Her mother scolds her. Shortly thereafter, the grandmother comes home as well. Look at the pictures and listen to the dialogue several times.

4

Listen to the entire dialogue once more, and answer the questions by marking the correct responses.

1. ¿A qué hora llega a casa Noelia?
   a. ■ A las doce de la noche.
   b. ■ A la una.
   c. ■ A las dos.

2. ¿Cómo fue la cena con Chema?
   a. ■ Fue una cena estupenda.
   b. ■ Fue una cena interesante.
   c. ■ Fue una cena aburrida.

3. ¿Qué le parece a Charo el regalo de Chema?
   a. ■ Muy práctico.
   b. ■ Muy bonito.
   c. ■ Poco romántico.

4. Charo está …
   a. ■ muy preocupada porque la abuela no ha llegado todavía.
   b. ■ enfadada porque la abuela no ha llamado.
   c. ■ nerviosa porque no sabe a quién llamar.

5. ¿Qué hizo la abuela por la noche?
   a. ■ Fue a dar un paseo con Noelia.
   b. ■ Fue a cenar a un restaurante.
   c. ■ Estuvo con las amigas tomando algo.

Seasons and months

5 TR. 62

Listen to the following sentences on the CD and repeat them. Then read the translations.

1. El restaurante era precioso.	a. *The restaurant was wonderful.*
2. La comida estaba muy buena.	b. *The meal was quite delicious.*
3. Es una broma.	c. *It's just a joke.*
4. No sé si llamar a la policía.	d. *I don't know whether to call the police.*
5. ¡Es un chico majísimo!	e. *He's a very nice boy!*
6. Yo era una chica muy bonita.	f. *I was a very pretty girl.*

6 TR. 61

Listen to the dialogue again and read along in the companion book. What expression in the dialogue means "okay"? Write it in the balloon.

If you wish, now you can read the translation of the dialogue in the companion book.

7 TR. 63

Listen to the CD to hear the words for the seasons and the months that are associated with them. Then match them with the appropriate pictures. Now you can listen to them again and repeat them.

1.   2.   3.   4.

Good to know:
Don't forget: In Spanish, the names of the months are not capitalized.

■ a. invierno: enero, febrero, marzo
■ b. verano: julio, agosto, septiembre
■ c. primavera: abril, mayo, junio
■ d. otoño: octubre, noviembre, diciembre

The ending -ísimo — Indefinite pronouns

8

▶ § 11 Comparisons

Take a look at the following sentence: **El restaurante estaba <u>llenísimo</u>.**
(The restaurant was extremely full.)

Good to know:

The endings **-ísimo /
-a / -os / -as** always
have a written accent
on the first **i**.

The ending **-ísimo** is attached to adjectives and expresses the absolute su-
perlative degree of comparison. Its endings change like those of any other
adjective ending in **-o**.
If the adjective ends in a consonant, **-ísimo** is added directly:

> **muy fácil ▶ facilísimo**

If the adjective ends in a vowel, replace the final vowel with **-ísimo:**

> **muy caro ▶ carísimo**   **muy grande ▶ grandísimo**

 2 TR. 64

Good to know:

Some adjectives
change their spelling
in order to preserve
the pronunciation:
**muy largo ▶
larguísimo
muy rico ▶ riquísimo**

Listen to the following sentences on the CD, and fill in the blanks with the
missing adjectives.

> 1. ¡Estábamos _____ !
>
> 2. ¡Es un chico _____ !
>
> 3. Cuando tenía tu edad, tenía _____ novios.

9

What single word would you use for each of the following expressions?
(f = feminine; m = masculine)

> 1. muy barato — 2. muy cansada — 3. muy elegante (*f*) — 4. muy fácil (*m*)

10

▶ § 32 Indefinite
   Pronouns

**Cuando tenía tu edad, tenía muchos novios, ¡muchísimos!:
uno para el lunes, otro para el martes, otro para el . . .**
The pronoun **uno** (*one, someone*) corresponds to the indefinite article **un**
without a noun. You will learn the other forms (feminine, singular, and plural) in the next exercise.

 2 TR. 65

Listen to the sentences and supply the missing forms.

> 1. No tengo aspirinas. ¿Tienes tú _____ ?
>
> 2. Yo siempre llevo gemelos. Ayer me regalaron _____ de oro.
>
> 3. Yo no necesito botas de montaña. Ya tengo _____ .

Diminutives — Personal direct objects

11

Diminutives are very popular in Spain as terms of endearment; they are formed by adding the ending **-ito / -ita**:
¿Nos pones una ración de <u>chopitos</u> (◀ chopo)?

The ending **-cito/ -cita** is used for words ending in **-e** or in a consonant:
¿Tomamos un <u>cafecito</u> (◀ café) aquí?

Note the possibility of a change in stress (see previous example)! Words that have **-z-** or **-c-** in the last syllable undergo the following orthographic changes: **-z- ▶ -c-** and **-c- ▶ -qu-**.

▶ **§ 8 Diminutives**

Good to know:
In Central America, as well as other parts of Latin America, the diminutive forms are very frequently used. One example is the name **Rosita** (◀ **Rosa**).

Now try to apply this rule yourself, and write the diminutive forms of the underlined words in the blanks.

    1. Nos hemos sentado en una <u>terraza</u> a tomar algo. _____

    2. Tienes un <u>poco</u> de fiebre. _____

12

The preposition **a** precedes the direct object if it is a person or a group of persons. Compare:
    ¿Has visto <u>a</u> la abuela?   **¿Has visto la película?**
    No sé si llamar <u>a</u> la policía.

▶ **§ 31 Direct Objects**

This also applies to pronouns that refer to persons, such as **quién, alguien** (*somebody*), **nadie**:
    ¿Habéis conocido <u>a</u> alguien en Salamanca?

Add the preposition **a** wherever it is needed.

    1. ¿Conoces ___ la mujer de Agustín?

    2. ¿ ___ quién has llamado?

    3. ¿Ve usted ___ la farmacia allí enfrente?

The preposition **a** is not used with **buscar** and **necesitar** + occupational designation:
La empresa busca una secretaria.
The same is true of the verb **tener** + indefinite article **un / una / unos / unas**:
Yo tengo una hermana.

The imperfect

13

▶ § 17 Imperfect

A new past tense form, the **imperfecto** (*imperfect*) appears in the main dialogue of this lesson:

Cuando <u>tenía</u> tu edad, yo <u>era</u> una chica muy bonita y me <u>encantaba</u> ir a bailar a las verbenas y <u>tenía</u> muchos novios, . . .

2 **TR. 66** Listen to and look at the regular imperfect forms for verbs ending in **-ar.** The example used is **estar.**

yo	est**aba**	nosotros/-as	est**ábamos**
tú	est**abas**	vosotros/-as	est**abais**
él/ella/usted	est**aba**	ellos/-as, ustedes	est**aban**

2 **TR. 67**

Now try to fill in the regular forms for verbs ending in **-er.** Use the CD to check your answers.

yo	ten**ía**	nosotros/-as	_____
tú	ten**ías**	vosotros/-as	ten**íais**
él/ella/usted	_____	ellos/-as, ustedes	ten**ían**

Good to know:

The imperfect of **hay** (*there is, there are*) is **había.**

Verbs ending in **–ir** are conjugated like verbs ending in **-er.** There are three irregular verbs in the imperfect: **Ser, ver, ir.**

ser: era, eras, era, éramos, erais, eran
ver: veía, veías, veía, veíamos, veíais, veían
ir: iba, ibas, iba, íbamos, ibais, iban

14

Doña Amparo tells here what life was like when she was young. Complete the sentences with the appropriate form in the imperfect tense.

cambiar — *to change*
antes — *before*
cuando — *when*
el vídeo — *videorecorder*
hoy en día — *nowadays*
numeroso / -a — *numerous*
fuera de — *besides*

¡Cómo ha cambiado todo! Antes, cuando yo (*ser*) _____ joven, no (*haber*) _____ ordenadores, ni horno microondas. La gente no (*ver*) _____ películas en vídeo, iba al cine, aunque no se (*salir*) _____ a cenar como hoy en día; se (*cenar*) _____ en casa. Las familias (*ser*) _____ muy numerosas y muy pocas mujeres (*trabajar*) _____ fuera de casa. Los chicos y las chicas no (*ir*) _____ a bailar a la discoteca, sino a la verbena. Mucha gente no (*tener*) _____ coche.

The use of the imperfect

15

The imperfect is used:

▶ § 17 Imperfect

a) to describe a condition or situation in the past, for example: **¡Estábamos preocupadísimas! El restaurante <u>era</u> precioso y la comida <u>estaba</u> muy buena.**

b) to describe customary or habitual past action: **Cuando tenía tu edad, <u>iba</u> a bailar a las verbenas.**

Function **a** or **b**? Enter the correct letter in each blank.

1. Cuando tenías mi edad, ¿qué hacías los fines de semana? _____

2. En Salamanca hacía muy buen tiempo. _____

In addition, the imperfect serves to describe a situation that forms the background for an interrupting action (the interrupting action is then in the preterit or present perfect):

… Y como la temperatura <u>era</u> tan agradable, nos hemos sentado en una terracita de la plaza a tomar algo.

16

What was it like when you were little? Answer the following questions in writing. You will find suggested answers in the companion book.

1. ¿Dónde vivía?
2. ¿Dónde pasaba los veranos?
3. ¿Le gustaba ir al colegio?
4. ¿Dónde jugaba con sus amigos/amigas?
5. ¿Qué no le gustaba hacer cuando era niño?
6. ¿Qué hacía los fines de semana?

Good to know:

The imperfect is also used to tell about your childhood:
cuando tenía seis años …, cuando era pequeño / -a / joven …, de niño/ -a … (*as a child …*).

17 TR. 68

Eva and María are chatting about their previous life as students. Listen to the dialogue. Which of the following statements apply to Eva, to María, or to both? Mark the correct answers.

		Eva	María
1.	Iba a la universidad por la mañana.		
2.	Tenía que trabajar tres días a la semana.		
3.	Vivía cerca de la universidad.		
4.	Vivía con su familia.		
5.	Ella y sus compañeras hacían muchas fiestas.		
6.	Tenía un novio que estudiaba en Barcelona.		
7.	A ella y a sus amigas les gustaba un compañero.		

*The weather in Spain — Intercultural tip: The **movida***

18  ✎

Listen to this conversation about a trip through Spain. Which regions of Spain are mentioned in connection with the weather illustrations? Match the numbers with the appropriate pictures.

A

B

C

D

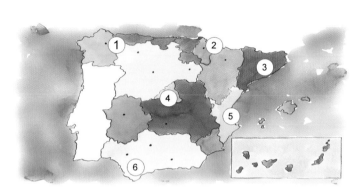

E

F

19

The **movida** had its origin in the period of the **transición** (the transition from dictatorship to democracy after Franco's death in 1975). It was a movement that ushered in a breaking of old taboos and the beginning of a new age. It pointed to new ways of doing things and brought progress to Spain with fresh ideas and enormous artistic potential. The **movida**—a concept that expresses the newfound enthusiasm for life and the new culture—came to refer particularly to nightlife.

Nightlife in Spain usually starts late and ends in the wee hours or even later the next morning. People start the evening on the **terrazas,** especially in summer, and friends and families as well enjoy these outdoor cafés.

Young people prefer to start nightlife later in the evening and go from one bar to the next. Places with live music are also popular. Usually substantial quantities of alcohol are consumed in the course of the evening. Then some people go on to the discos to finish out the "evening" (possibly around 5 A.M.!).

Those who have more energy can keep going until dawn, when they greet the new day in a café with **churros con chocolate** (*thin tubes of deep-fried dough with hot chocolate*).

Mexican dishes — Expressing surprise

1

The following short dialogues have to do with Mexican foods. Listen to the dialogues, and first concentrate on picking out the names of the dishes mentioned. Then look at the explanations of the dishes given below. Listen to the dialogues again, and try to identify the individual words of the definitions as well.

1. pollo con mole
2. quesadilla
3. enchilada
4. chile con carne
5. pozole
6. burrito

Mole: *Sauce with chile peppers, various seasonings, peanuts, and chocolate*
Quesadilla: *Corn tortilla filled with cheese or other ingredients*
Enchilada: *Rolled-up corn tortilla filled with meat and covered with a chile-pepper sauce*
Chile con carne: *Typical Tex-Mex dish with chile peppers, meat, and beans*
Pozole: *Dish made with corn, meat, and chile peppers*
Burrito: *Rolled-up flour tortilla filled with beef or chicken, beans, rice, and other ingredients*

Good to know:
The term **Tex-Mex** refers to a blend of the eating customs of Texas and Mexico, brought about by the to-and-fro movement between the two regions.

2

On the CD, listen to the following ways of expressing surprise, and repeat them. Can you find the translation that matches each expression?

1. ¡Qué sorpresa!
2. ¡Qué tarde es!
3. No me lo puedo creer.
4. ¿De verdad?
5. ¡No me digas!
6. ¡Me parece que estoy soñando!
7. ¡Qué pronto habéis llegado!
8. ¡Esto sí que no me lo esperaba!
9. ¿Ah, sí?
10. ¡No puede ser verdad!

a. *How quickly you've gotten here!*
b. *I must be dreaming!*
c. *How late it is!*
d. *You don't say!*
e. *Oh, yes?*
f. *It can't be true!*
g. *I wouldn't have expected this!*
h. *Really?*
i. *I can't believe it!*
j. *What a surprise!*

At a Mexican restaurant

3

This evening Mr. and Mrs. Giménez are going out to eat. They want to try a new Mexican restaurant. A surprise awaits them there. Look at the pictures, and listen to the dialogue several times.

4

Listen to the dialogue again. Then decide whether the following statements are true or false.

		correcto	falso
1.	A Agustín no le gusta la decoración del restaurante.		
2.	Charo no sabe lo que son los burritos.		
3.	Agustín quiere hablar primero con el camarero.		
4.	Agustín y Charo estuvieron una vez en Thailandia.		
5.	Charo tiene mucha hambre.		
6.	Rosita comenta que viajar a México es muy caro.		
7.	Rosita trabaja en el restaurante todos los días.		
8.	Charo quiere cenar pollo con mole.		

At the restaurant

5

Listen to the following expressions and repeat them. Can you match each with its correct translation?

1. ¡Qué bien decorado está este restaurante!

2. ¿Qué son burritos?

3. ¡Venga!, vamos a pedir.

4. ¡Vaya! ¡Pero si es Rosita!

5. ¡Qué sorpresa!

6. ¡Pensaba que trabajabas en un museo!

7. ¡Chocolate en una salsa y con pollo!

8. ¡Qué original!

9. ¿Qué tal si eliges tú?

10. ¡Pues sí ...!

a. *I thought you worked in a museum!*

b. *What a surprise!*

c. *How odd!*

d. *What are* **burritos**?

e. *Well!*

f. *Chocolate in a sauce, and with chicken!*

g. *How well decorated this restaurant is!*

h. *Come on! That's just Rosita!*

i. *Come on, let's order.*

j. *How about if you choose?*

6

Listen to the dialogue and read along in the companion book. Rosita uses a new word for "money" in the dialogue. Can you find it? Write it in the balloon below.

Now underline the verbs in the text that are in the imperfect tense. Then look at the translation of the entire dialogue.

Good to know:
Do you remember? In Latin American countries, **ustedes** is always used in place of **vosotros**. That's why Rosita says **¿Les gusta la comida mexicana?** (*Do you like Mexican food?*) using the familiar pronoun for Charo and Agustín individually.

Irregular forms in the preterit

7

▶ § 16 Preterit
(Indefinido)

Look at Charo's question from the dialogue.
¿Recuerdas cuando pedimos sin saber qué eran las cosas?
(Do you remember when we ordered without knowing what the things were?)

In verbs ending in **–ir** that undergo a vowel change in the present tense
(such as **pe̱dir ▶ yo pi̱do, dive̱rtirse ▶ yo me divi̱erto**), the stem vowel also
changes from **e** to **i** in the preterit as well, but only in the third person singular and plural.

Look at the preterit forms of **pedir**.

yo	pedí	nosotros, nosotras	ped-**imos**
tú	ped-**iste**	vosotros, vosotras	ped-**isteis**
él, ella, usted	pid-**ió**	ellos, ellas, ustedes	pid-**ieron**

In the following exercise, try to conjugate **divertirse**, following the pattern
of **pedir**. Write the missing forms in the blanks.

yo	me divertí	nosotros/-as	nos divertimos
tú	te divertiste	vosotros/-as	os divertisteis
él, ella, usted	_____	ellos, ellas, ustedes	_____

8

▶ § 16 Preterit
(Indefinido)

In the dialogue, Agustín uses some additional irregular preterit forms.
**Tú no _quisiste_ quedarte en el hotel y _propusiste_ salir en busca de aventu-
ras.** *(You didn't want to stay in the hotel and suggested going out in search
of adventures.)*

The verbs **querer** *(to want)* and **proponer** *(to suggest)* have an irregular
stem in the preterit:

querer ▶ quis-	proponer ▶ propus-

The endings are the same as for the verb **hacer,** which you will find in the
conjugation box on the left.

Preterit of hacer

hice	hicimos
hiciste	hicisteis
hizo	hicieron

Try to fill in the blanks in the conjugation box on the left with the appropriate preterit forms of **querer.**

Preterit of querer

_____	quisimos
quisiste	_____
_____	_____

quisieron — quise — quiso — quisisteis

Imperfect vs. preterit

9

As you learned in the last lesson, the imperfect is also used to describe the circumstances or the background of a main action. The main action is then in the preterit or present perfect.

▶ § 16 Preterit
(Indefinido)

▶ § 17 Imperfect

2
TR. 74

In the following sentence, note the tense of each verb and its context. Listen to the sentence on the CD, and then supply the missing verbs.

> Al principio _____ toda la semana, pero era demasiado para
>
> mí; entonces _____ pensar un poco más en mi salud.

The imperfect frequently appears with information such as **antes** (*previously*), **siempre, todos los días, mientras** (*while*), etc.

The preterit, however, is often used with information such as **entonces, de repente** (*suddenly*), **de pronto** (*all at once*), **enseguida** (*immediately*), **un día** (*one day*).

Good to know:
The imperfect answers the question *What was it like?* The preterit and present perfect answer the question *What happened?*

10 ✎

This is the short version of the legend of the accidental discovery of the Mexican sauce **mole.** Look at the preterit and imperfect forms in parentheses, and fill in each blank with the correct form. Then you can read the translation of the legend in the companion book.

Un día el arzobispo de Puebla (*decidió / decidía*) _____ visitar uno de

los conventos de la zona. Los monjes entonces (*comenzaron / comenzaban*)

_____ a preparar la comida. Fray Pascual (*se puso / se ponía*)

_____ a recoger los chiles, trozos de chocolate y las especias que

(*hubo / había*) _____ por la cocina. Con las prisas

(*tropezó / tropezaba*) _____ frente a la cazuela donde se

(*estuvo / estaba*) _____ haciendo la comida.

Poco después (*llegó / llegaba*) _____ el arzobispo. Cuando

(*probó / probaba*) _____ la comida, (*exclamó / exclamaba*)

_____ : "¡Exquisito!"

Good to know:
Puebla is the capital of the state of the same name in central Mexico.

A story in pictures — Imperfect vs. preterit

11

Listen to the story about Jordi's grandfather and put the pictures in chronological order by numbering them from 1 to 6.

12

> ▶ § 16 Preterit
> (Indefinido)

> ▶ § 17 Imperfect

aparecer — *to seem, to appear*
atender — *to wait on*
explicar — *to explain*
al final — *in the end*
el guiso — *(cooked) dish*

Here is an excerpt from Charo's diary. Fill in the blanks in the text with the preterit or imperfect of the verb given. Remember that you need to conjugate the verbs in the first person plural (**nosotros**) if they describe actions by Charo and her husband.

Ayer Agustín y yo (*ir*) _____ a cenar a un restaurante mexicano.

(*haber*) _____ un ambiente muy agradable. Allí (*ver*) _____ a

Rosita, nuestra vecina. (*estar*) _____ esperando al camarero, cuando

de repente (*aparecer*) _____ ella para atendernos. ¡Qué sorpresa! Muy

amablemente nos (*explicar*) _____ lo que (*ser*) _____ todo y nos

(*ayudar*) _____ a elegir la cena. Al final (*tomar*) _____ pozole,

un guiso que (*estar*) _____ riquísimo.

13

Find the **imperfect—preterit** pairs of the following verbs and write them down.

quería	propusiste	proponíamos	pedisteis
se divirtió	quise	pedíais	quisieron
proponías	se divertía	propusimos	querían

Expressing surprise — Mexican dishes

14 ✎

Connect the sentences on the left with the appropriate replies on the right.

¡Hola, Agustín!

1.

A

¡No me digas! Pero, ¿cómo ha sido?

Creo que he perdido la cartera.

2.

B

¡Esto sí que no me lo esperaba!

Jordi y yo queremos darte este regalo.

3.

C

¡Manolo! ¡Qué sorpresa! ¿Cómo estás?

15  ✎

Read the following definitions of Mexican dishes. Can you match them with the appropriate names of dishes on the right? Then use the CD to check your answers.

1. Es una tortilla de maíz rellena de carne y cubierta con salsa de chile.

     a. mole

2. Es un guiso de maíz con carne y chile.

     b. burritos

3. Es un plato de carne, chile y frijoles.

     c. pozole

4. Es una salsa hecha con chile, muchas especias, cacahuetes y chocolate.

     d. quesadillas

5. Son tortillas de maíz rellenas de queso y muchas otras cosas.

     e. enchilada

6. Son tortillas de trigo enrolladas, rellenas de carne, pollo y otros ingredientes.

     f. chile con carne

◀ **cubierto/a** — *covered*
el chile — *chile pepper*
el plato — *dish*
enrollado/a — *rolled up*

Role play — Intercultural tip: Corn

16 🖉

Charo tells her daughter, Noelia, about the dinner in a Mexican restaurant. Listen to the dialogue between Charo and Noelia several times. Then play the role of Charo, and complete the dialogue.

You tell her that last night you had dinner in a Mexican restaurant, but you can't remember its name.

_____

_____

Noelia: ¿Puebla?
You say that's the right name: _____
Noelia: ¿Y qué tal?
You tell what it was like and say that you met someone: _____

_____

Noelia: ¿A quién?
You met Rosita, the neighbor: _____
Noelia: Ah, sí, es verdad. Está trabajando allí de camarera, ¿no?
You ask how Noelia knows that: _____
Noelia: Porque me lo comentó el otro día.
You say you were just waiting for the waiter when Rosita suddenly appeared to serve you:

_____

_____

Noelia: Bueno, ¿y qué comisteis?
*You say that you ate **pozole**:* _____
Noelia: Po … ¿qué?
*You explain what **pozole** is and describe how it tasted:* _____

_____

_____

17

Corn did not reach Europe until the fifteenth century, when America was discovered. This grain was very widespread in Central and South America and was the most important item in the diet of the great pre-Columbian civilizations:
- the **Aztecs:** In central Mexico
- the **Maya:** In southeastern Mexico, the Yucatán, and Guatemala
- the **Incas:** Their region included southern Colombia, Ecuador, Peru, Bolivia, northwestern Argentina, and a large part of Chile.

Mexico has 22 different kinds of corn, which serve as the basis for production of a large number of foods.

Intercultural Tip

Stating plans and intentions — A language school

1

Look at these pictures. What plans or intentions do these people have? Match the sentences with the appropriate pictures, and use the CD to check your answers.

Good to know:
Use **querer / pensar / ir a** + infinitive to express intentions:
quiero ir al cine
pienso ir al cine
voy a ir al cine

1.
2.
3.

4.
5.

a. Mi mujer y yo pensamos salir a cenar esta noche. — b. El próximo verano quiero viajar a México. — c. Esta tarde pienso llamar por teléfono a mi madre. — d. Este fin de semana voy a ir al cine. — e. Mañana voy a dar un paseo con mis amigas.

2

Read the advertisement (**el anuncio**) for a Spanish language school. Then look at the English terms on the right, and try to find their Spanish equivalents in the ad and underline them.

Good to know:
D.E.L.E. stands for **Diploma de Español como Lengua Extranjera** (*Diploma in Spanish as a Foreign Language*). These are state-issued diplomas attesting to the level of linguistic competence achieved.

ENMADRID — Cursos de Español para Extranjeros

¡Aprende español en la capital de España!

Cursos durante todo el año de 2 semanas hasta 9 meses
10 tipos de cursos
Preparación para los Diplomas D.E.L.E. de inicial a superior
Máximo 10 estudiantes por clase
Material de clase incluido en la matrícula
Alojamiento: familias, apartamentos, residencia propia
Amplio programa de actividades: deportes, excursiones, visitas, …

reservation
registration
course
accommodations

ENMADRID — C/ Marqués de Cubas, 2 — 28014 Madrid
Información y reserva: Tel.: +34 915 245 765
Fax: +34 915 235 771
E-mail: cursos@enmadrid.es
http://www.enmadrid.com

Doña Amparo's secret

3

There's a reason for Doña Amparo's frequent escapades. During a family dinner, Doña Amparo tells her family some happy news, and thus the truth comes to light. Look at the pictures and listen to the dialogue.

4

Listen to the dialogue again, and then match the statements with the correct speaker.

conseguir —
to obtain
ganado ◀ **ganar** —
to win
cogido ◀ **coger** —
to take
las vacaciones —
vacation
celebrar —
to celebrate

1.

2.

- ▨ a. Ha comprado varias cosas en la perfumería.
- ▨ b. No sabe cómo conseguir el dinero.
- ▨ c. Piensa ahorrar un poco de dinero.
- ▨ d. Quiere hacer un curso de inglés.
- ▨ e. Ha ganado mucho dinero en el bingo.
- ▨ f. Va a hacer la reserva mañana.
- ▨ g. Ha cogido dinero del bolso de Charo.
- ▨ h. Quiere irse de vacaciones con las amigas.
- ▨ i. Propone celebrar el dinero ganado en el bingo.

5

Listen to the following sentences and repeat them.

generoso/a —
generous
desaparecer —
to disappear

1. ¿No querías hacer un curso de inglés?
2. ¿Pero qué pasa que está tan generosa?
3. Ahora entiendo por qué me desaparecía dinero.
4. Quiero irme a Benidorm con mis amigas.
5. ¡Vamos a celebrar el bingo de la abuela!

Stating plans and intentions

6

Listen to the dialogue again, and read along in the companion book. In the text, mark the plans or intentions of Doña Amparo and Noelia.
What word does Doña Amparo use to apologize? Write it in the balloon—it's just one word!

If you wish, you can finish reading the translation of the dialogue in the companion book.

7

It's Friday evening: Noelia, Rosita, Jordi, and Chema are talking about their plans for the next day.
First, read the sentences. Then listen to the dialogue. To whom do these statements apply? Mark the answers. A statement can also apply to several people.

		Chema	Jordi	Noelia	Rosita
1.	Piensa hacer deporte.				
2.	Va a salir con unos amigos.				
3.	Tiene que ayudar en casa.				
4.	Quiere ir de compras.				
5.	Va a ir a bailar.				
6.	Tiene que trabajar.				
7.	Va a ir al cine con unos amigos.				

Stating plans and intentions

8

Good to know:

Please note: In the verbs **querer, tener,** and **pensar**, the stem vowel **e** changes to **ie** in all forms except the first and second person plural.

Look at the following constructions and their use.

• To express an intention, use **querer** (*to want; to like*) + infinitive:
  Quiero irme de vacaciones a Benidorm.
• To express a wish and thus possibly an intention, use **tener ganas de** (*to wish to*) + infinitive:
  Tenemos ganas de pasear por la playa.
• To state an intention or a plan for the near future, use **ir a** + infinitive:
  Mañana voy a hacer la reserva en la academia.
• You can also use **pensar** (*to intend*) to state an intention or a plan:
  Pienso ahorrar un poquito.

9

Match the plans and intentions below with the appropriate pictures. Check your answers with the help of the CD.

remar — *to row*
la barbacoa — *barbecue, grill party*
el jardín — *garden*

1.   2.   3.

a. Mi jefe va a hacer una barbacoa en el jardín este domingo.
b. Mis compañeros y yo pensamos ir a remar al Retiro.
c. El próximo verano pienso descansar y no hacer nada.

10

And what plans do you have? Answer the following questions. You will find suggested answers in the companion book.

1. ¿Qué va a hacer el próximo sábado por la noche?
2. ¿Dónde piensa pasar sus próximas vacaciones?
3. ¿Qué quiere hacer el próximo año?
4. ¿Qué tiene ganas de hacer después del trabajo?

*Placement of pronouns — **ser** and **estar***

11

With an infinitive, pronouns can either precede the verb or be attached:
Me quiero ir de vacaciones.
Quiero ir<u>me</u> de vacaciones.

The same thing is true for **tener que** + infinitive:
Tengo que ir<u>me</u>.
Me tengo que ir.

And for **estar** + present participle:

Rosita está acostándo<u>se</u>.
Rosita <u>se</u> está acostando.

▶ **§ 29 Placement of Pronouns**

Good to know:
A written accent must always be used when a pronoun is attached to a present participle, to preserve the stress:
leyendo ▶ leyéndolo

Write the following sentences in a different way.

1. Mañana me tengo que levantar temprano.

2. ¿Te estás afeitando, Agustín?

12

To express essentially lasting features of character or appearance, use **ser** + adjective: **Doña Amparo <u>es</u> muy <u>amable</u>.**

To express a temporary condition or an accidental or occasional feature, use **estar** + adjective: **Doña Amparo <u>está contenta</u>.**

Now look at the following sentence from the dialogue:
Pero, abuela, ¿qué pasa que está tan generosa?
(But Grandmother, what's going on, why so generous?)
Doña Amparo's particular generosity is depicted here as a thing of the moment, not as an inherent trait of hers. Therefore the verb **estar**, rather than **ser**, is used.

▶ **§ 19 ser / estar**

Good to know:
Some adjectives have different meanings, depending on whether they are used with **ser** or **estar**, as in these examples:
estar cansado/a
— to be tired
ser cansado/a *— to be tiring*, as in **un viaje cansado**

Choose the correct verb for each sentence below, and fill in the blanks.

1. Mi jefe es bastante antipático pero hoy (*ha estado / ha sido*)

   _____ muy simpático.

2. Carmen, ¡(*eres / estás*) _____ muy delgada!

   ¡Tienes que comer más!

ser and *estar* — *Prepositions of time*

13

▶ § 19 ser / estar

Ser or **estar**? Fill in the blanks in the following dialogues, using the correct verbs. Always pay attention to the context!

1. • (*soy / estoy*) _____ muy nervioso.

    ○ ¿Cómo puede ser? ¡Si tú (*eres / estás*) _____ una persona muy

       tranquila!

2. • ¿Qué tal la fiesta de cumpleaños?

    ○ (*ha sido / ha estado*) _____ muy bien.

3. • (*eres / estás*) _____ muy seria hoy. ¿Te pasa algo?

    ○ Me duele mucho la cabeza.

4. • ¿Y cómo (*es / está*) _____ él?

    ○ ¡(*es / está*) _____ un chico fascinante! ¡Tienes que conocerlo!

14

▶ § 37 Prepositions

Take a look at the following expressions and sample sentences.
· **hace** + period of time *(ago)*:
   hace tres días / hace cinco meses / hace diez años / . . .
   Empezamos <u>hace</u> <u>medio año</u> **aproximadamente.**
· **desde** + point in time *(since)*:
   desde ayer / desde hoy / desde marzo / desde 2002 / . . .
   Mis amigas y yo vamos al bingo <u>desde</u> <u>abril</u>**.**
· **desde hace** + period of time *(for)*:
   desde hace tres días / desde hace cinco meses / desde hace diez años / . . .
   Mis amigas y yo vamos al bingo <u>desde hace</u> <u>medio año</u>**.**

TR. 83

Good to know:

Some verbs are spelled differently in the imperfect tense to preserve their pronunciation, for example, **llegar: (yo) llegué**

Put these words in the correct blanks, and use the CD to check your answers.

desde — hace — desde hace

1. Estoy trabajando en este proyecto _____ el año pasado.

2. No veo a mi familia _____ meses.

3. Llegué a Madrid _____ un año.

Prepositions of time — Stressed and unstressed possessive adjectives

15

Use **hace**, **desde**, or **desde hace** to complete the sentences below.

▶ § 37 Prepositions

    1. ¡No vamos al cine _____ diez años!

    2. Rosita trabaja en este museo _____ el pasado octubre.

    3. Estuve hablando con él _____ unos días.

    4. Viven aquí _____ un par de meses.

    5. _____ hoy trabajo en un nuevo departamento.

16

The stressed possessive adjectives can be used with or without a definite article:

▶ § 34 Possessive Adjectives

    Tus amigas no van al bingo, pero <u>las mías</u> sí.
    Este dinero es <u>tuyo</u>, Charo.

Listen to the dialogue and fill in the missing expression.

    Charo: Pero Amparo, coger dinero del bolso, a su edad …

    Amparo: Ya lo sé, _____ .

The stressed forms follow the noun when special emphasis is placed on the possessive adjective:

    Yo no conozco a esas amigas <u>tuyas</u>.

The unstressed possessive adjectives always precede the noun:

    Noelia es <u>mi</u> nieta.

You can find all the forms of the stressed and unstressed possessive adjectives in the Grammar section of the companion book.

> **Good to know:**
> In certain exclamations such as ¡**Dios mío!** (*my God!*) and in expressions such as **hijo mío** (*my boy*) and **amigo mío** (*my friend*), the stressed possessive adjectives follow the noun.

17

Complete the sentences with the appropriate form.

1. Y (*sus / suyos*) _____ hijos, ¿qué estudian?

2. Ayer conocí a un primo (*tu / tuyo*) _____ .

3. ¿Dónde tienes (*tus / tuyas*) _____ cosas?

4. (*mis / mías*) _____ gafas están aquí, pero no veo las (*tus / tuyas*) _____ .

5. Ana es amiga (*su / suya*) _____ , ¿no?

A puzzle — Intercultural tip: Spanish lotteries

18 ✏

Put the puzzle parts together in pairs to form complete sentences or questions.

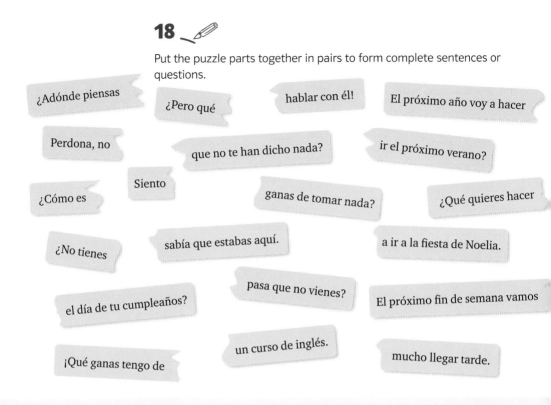

¿Adónde piensas

¿Pero qué

hablar con él!

El próximo año voy a hacer

Perdona, no

que no te han dicho nada?

ir el próximo verano?

Siento

¿Cómo es

ganas de tomar nada?

¿Qué quieres hacer

¿No tienes

sabía que estabas aquí.

a ir a la fiesta de Noelia.

el día de tu cumpleaños?

pasa que no vienes?

El próximo fin de semana vamos

un curso de inglés.

¡Qué ganas tengo de

mucho llegar tarde.

19

In addition to bingo, other games of chance are very popular in Spain. The oldest and most important is the **Lotería Nacional.** The traditional **Sorteo Extraordinario de Navidad** (*Special Christmas Lottery*) is held every year on December 12. The grand prize, that is, the winning ticket, is called **El Gordo** (literally: *the Fat One*). Few can resist the temptation to buy a ticket, a tenth of a ticket, or a smaller share.

Another lottery takes place on a daily basis: **El Cupón de la ONCE (Organización Nacional de Ciegos Españoles)** (*National Organization for the Blind of Spain*).

In addition, the **Lotería Primitiva** and the **Bonoloto** are quite popular. They involve combinations of certain numbers. The **Quiniela de fútbol** (*a soccer betting game*) is also very widely played, of course.

TR. 85

In this picture you see two tenths of tickets for the **Lotería Nacional.** Choose one, and then listen to see whether you've won!

A trip to Mexico — Computer-related vocabulary

1

On the CD, listen to a commercial for trips to the Yucatán in Mexico, and read the words mentioned in the commercial in the order given. Then match the translations below with their Spanish equivalents.

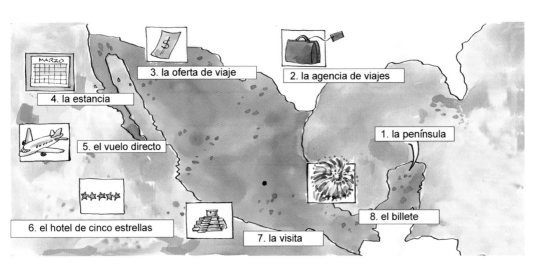

3. la oferta de viaje
2. la agencia de viajes
4. la estancia
1. la península
5. el vuelo directo
8. el billete
6. el hotel de cinco estrellas
7. la visita

■ a. *travel offering* — ■ b. *ticket* — ■ c. *five-star hotel* — ■ d. *travel agency* — ■ e. *visit* — ■ f. *stay* — ■ g. *direct flight* — ■ h. *peninsula*

2

Listen to the sentences on the CD and repeat them. Can you match them with their English equivalents?

Good to know:
The word **emilio** is a colloquial term for e-mail. You can also use the expression **correo electrónico** or just the English word **e-mail**.

1. A ella le encanta navegar por internet.
2. Vamos a introducir primero el CD-ROM.
3. Tengo que enviar un par de "emilios".
4. ¿Por qué no miras en ese portal?
5. ¿Sabéis cómo instalar el nuevo programa?
6. La pantalla es un poco pequeña.
7. Él es un experto en informática.
8. El ordenador se ha colgado otra vez.

a. *He's an IT expert.*
b. *The computer has crashed again.*
c. *Why don't you look at that home page?*
d. *The screen is a little small.*
e. *First we'll insert the CD-ROM.*
f. *Do you know how to install the new program?*
g. *I have to send a couple of e-mails.*
h. *She loves to surf the Internet.*

Noelia and Chema's trip

3

It's clear that Noelia and Chema are more than friends. Noelia is in Chema's room. They are sitting in front of the computer and trying to make reservations on the Internet for a trip to Mexico. Look at the pictures and listen to the dialogue several times.

4

Listen to the dialogue, and then answer the questions by marking each correct response.

I. ¿Qué lugares deciden visitar Noelia y Chema?
a. ◼ Ciudad de México.
b. ◼ Uxmal, Chichén-Itzá y Tulúm.
c. ◼ Yucatán y Ciudad de México.

---

salir — *to leave*
durar — *to last*
utilizar — *to use*

---

2. ¿A qué hora sale el avión de Madrid?
a. ◼ A las doce y media de la mañana.
b. ◼ A las dos y media de la mañana.
c. ◼ A las dos y media de la tarde.

3. ¿Cuántas horas dura el vuelo a México?
a. ◼ Casi doce horas.
b. ◼ Casi once horas.
c. ◼ Cinco horas y cuarto.

4. ¿Cuántas estrellas tiene el hotel de Mérida?
a. ◼ Dos.
b. ◼ Tres.
c. ◼ Cuatro.

5. ¿Para qué utiliza Chema el ordenador de casa?
a. ◼ Sólo para navegar por internet.
b. ◼ Sólo para escribir "emilios".
c. ◼ Para escribir "emilios" y navegar por internet.

Surfing the Internet — Calling the travel agency

5   TR. 89

Listen to the following sentences on the CD and repeat them. Then look at the translations below.

1. Vamos a seguir buscando.
2. ¡Ay, qué lento es este ordenador!
3. ¡Ah, pero el vuelo no está incluido!
4. Vamos a mirar en el portal de Iberia.
5. ¡Se me ha colgado el ordenador! ¡Qué fastidio!

a. *Let's keep looking.*
b. *Oh, how slow this computer is!*
c. *Oh, but the flight is not included!*
d. *Let's look at the Iberia home page.*
e. *The computer has crashed! How annoying!*

6 TR. 88

Listen to the dialogue and read along in the companion book. Now underline the three sentences that contain a comparison.
Then write in the balloon below the method of payment you can use to pay on the Internet.

7 TR. 90

Agustín calls a travel agency to buy an airline ticket. Listen to the dialogue on the CD, and mark the statements below that apply to the conversation.

1. Agustín llama por teléfono a la agencia de viajes "Hispania".
2. Agustín quiere viajar a Sevilla el próximo fin de semana.
3. Agustín piensa viajar solo.
4. El vuelo sale de Madrid a las seis y diez de la tarde.
5. El vuelo dura más o menos una hora.
6. El billete de avión cuesta 150 euros.
7. Agustín tiene que ir a la agencia antes del jueves.
8. Agustín prefiere pagar con tarjeta de crédito.

seguir + present participle — The relative pronouns *el / la / los / las que*

8

▶ § 18 Present Participle

Good to know:

The verb **seguir** is irregular. The vowel in the stem **seg-** changes to **sig-** for all persons except the first and second person plural.

You already know the verb **pasar** (*to spend, as time*) with its present participle. The present participle can also be used with other verbs that express duration or continuation of an action, such as **seguir** (*to continue; to keep on*).

2 TR. 91

On the CD, listen to what Chema says, and fill in the blank in the sentence below with the missing word.

> Vamos a seguir _____ , a ver si encontramos algo.

If the sentence contains a direct object pronoun, this pronoun either precedes the verb **seguir** or is attached to the present participle:

> **Lo sigo buscando. / Sigo buscándolo.**

Good to know:

If the pronoun is attached to the present participle, a written accent is required, so that the stress remains on the same syllable of the verb.

9

Complete the text of the e-mail that Chema is writing to his friend.

¡Hola, Borja! ¡Noelia y yo nos vamos a México! Bueno, de momento estamos

mirando _____ de _____ en internet. Hoy hemos encontrado una

realmente interesante con _____ en hotel de cuatro _____ pero,

claro, el _____ no estaba incluido. Vamos a tener que seguir buscando

porque sin vuelo _____ , va a ser mucho más caro.

¡Hasta el próximo _____ !

10

▶ § 35 Relative Pronouns

Good to know:

The expression **lo que** means *that which* or *what*: ¿**Sabes lo que pasa?** (*Do you know what is happening?*)

El / la / los / las que are relative pronouns that are used for things and persons. They are a combination of the definite article and **que**:

> **El que tengo en la oficina es mucho mejor.**
> (*The one I have in the office is much better.*)

El / la / los / las que are also used with prepositions.

2 TR. 92

Listen to the following sentence on the CD, and fill in the blank with the missing words.

> ¡Por fin vamos a ver las pirámides **de** _____ tanto
> nos ha hablado Rosita!

Placing the direct object first — The dative of interest

11

Compare the following sentences:

Utilizo <u>este ordenador</u> sólo para navegar por internet.
<u>Este ordenador, lo</u> utilizo sólo para navegar por internet.

> ▶ § 26 Direct Object
> Pronouns

If the direct object (here: **ordenador**) precedes the verb, it must be repeated in the form of the appropriate direct object pronoun (here: **lo**). The direct object is placed first for emphasis.

> **Good to know:**
>
> Frequently a direct object that is placed first is followed by a comma, but it is not absolutely necessary.

Put these direct object pronouns in the correct blanks.

> la — lo — las — los

1. Estos billetes, _____ ha pagado la abuela.

2. A tu amiga mexicana, _____ visitamos, ¿no?

3. Las vacaciones, _____ podemos pasar aquí.

4. El viaje, _____ vamos a hacer este año.

12

Look at Chema's words, taken from the dialogue:

> **¡Se <u>me</u> ha colgado el ordenador!**
> *(The computer has crashed!)*

> ▶ § 30 Dative of Interest

Chema could also have said:

> **¡Se ha colgado el ordenador!**

The pronoun **me** is called a **dative of interest** (**dativo de interés**). Its function is to show the speaker's interest in what is happening or has happened to him or someone else. This expresses the involvement and concern of the speaker with regard to the event.

For review, take a look at all the indirect object pronouns again:

me   te   le   nos   os   les

With the help of the words in parentheses, complete the following sentence with the correct pronoun.

> ¡Se (*a nosotros*) _____ ha colgado el ordenador!

At the hotel — Reserving a room

13

Here you see sentences that are used in situations at a hotel. Listen to them on the CD and repeat them. Then match each one with its English equivalent.

1. Quisiera reservar una habitación doble.
2. ¿Tiene aire acondicionado la habitación?
3. ¿Me puede dejar su carnet de identidad?
4. ¿Tienen habitaciones libres para esta noche?
5. ¿Está incluido el desayuno en el precio?
6. ¿Tienen habitaciones individuales?

a. *Does the room have air-conditioning?*
b. *Do you have single rooms?*
c. *Can you give me your identification card?*
d. *Is breakfast included in the price?*
e. *I would like to reserve a double room.*
f. *Do you have any vacant rooms for tonight?*

14

Read the e-mail that Agustín wrote to a hotel to reserve a room. Then fill in the blanks with the correct words. Were you able to guess the meanings of the unfamiliar words from the context? Compare your guesses with the translations below.

Good to know:

Spanish double rooms (**la habitación doble**) have both separate beds (**camas individuales / separadas**) and double beds (**la cama matrimonial**). Therefore, it is always a good idea to inquire in advance.

atentamente — aparcamiento — doble — nombre — reservar — estimados — restaurante

_____ señores:

Mi _____ es Agustín Giménez. Me gustaría _____ en su hotel una habitación _____ con cama matrimonial para los días 23 y 24 del presente mes. También me gustaría saber si el hotel dispone de servicio de _____ y de _____ propio.

Les saluda _____ ,

Agustín Giménez

el nombre — *name*
presente — *present, current*
disponer — *to have available*
Estimados señores — *Dear Sirs*
Les saluda atentamente — *Yours sincerely*

el servicio — *service*
el aparcamiento — *parking lot, garage*
propio/a — *own*

Making a phone call

15

In Spain, **¿Diga? / ¿Dígame?** is the customary way of answering the phone as an individual (businesses, of course, state the company's name). In Mexico, however, people say **¡Bueno!** when they answer the phone.

Here you see a few appropriate phrases to use on the phone. Listen to them on the CD and read along.

To ask to speak to someone:
> **Hola, ¿está Agustín?**
> **Quería hablar con el señor Giménez.**

To ask for information:
> **Por favor, ¿me da el número de teléfono del hotel Alcora en Sevilla?**

To ask who is calling:
> **¿De parte de quién?**

To pass the phone to the person the call is for:
> **Sí, ahora se pone.**
> **Sí, un momento, no cuelgue.**

To say that the caller has a wrong number:
> **Se ha equivocado.**
> **No es aquí.**

Listen to the telephone conversation between Charo and a caller on the CD. Then play the role of Charo and complete the dialogue.

You answer the telephone: _____

> *Caller:* Hola, buenos días. Quería hablar con el señor Giménez.

You ask who is calling: _____

> *Caller:* Soy Alejandro Cifuentes.

You ask him to wait a minute and say that the person he wants is coming to the

phone: _____

_____

> *Caller:* Gracias.

A crossword puzzle — Intercultural tip: The Yucatán Peninsula

16 ✎

Can you solve the crossword puzzle? Put your answers in the appropriate squares.

1. Algo que se puede instalar en el ordenador.
2. Una parte del ordenador.
3. A los expertos en … les encantan los ordenadores.
4. Otra palabra para e-mail.
5. Una actividad que se hace por internet.
6. Cuando el ordenador no sigue funcionando decimos que se ha …
7. Muchas agencias de viajes tienen en internet su propio …

17

The classical Maya culture developed in the first centuries A.D. in southeastern Mexico, Guatemala, Belize, Honduras, and El Salvador. At the highpoint of this civilization, around 750 A.D., experts estimate that between three and thirteen million people settled in the lowlands of the Yucatán peninsula alone. The Yucatán is now part of Mexico.

Mayan culture was in many respects the most highly developed of all the ancient American cultures. The Mayans had a complex writing system, an accurate calendar, and some knowledge of astronomy.

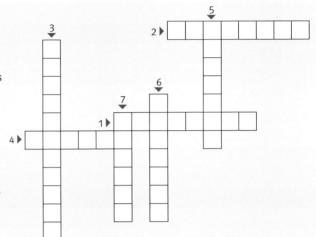

The culture of the Mayans survives today on the Yucatán peninsula, where the Mayan language is spoken and people continue to practice old customs and traditions. In the midst of the present-day Mayan culture stand the ceremonial centers of the old master builders with their impressive pyramidal temples, such as **Uxmal, Tulúm** (not far from the modern-day tourist area of **Cancún**), and **Chichén-Itzá**, the former capital of the Yucatán.

The present capital of the Yucatán is **Mérida,** founded in 1542, famed for its cathedrals and the old historic quarters.

Intercultural Tip

Replying properly — Describing feelings and moods

1

Match the Spanish sentences on the right with their correct paraphrases on the left. Then use the CD to check your answers, and repeat the sentences out loud.

1. *describing a past habit*

2. *on the telephone, asking who is calling*

3. *stating an intention*

4. *expressing surprise*

5. *making a reservation at a hotel*

a. Quisiera reservar una habitación doble.

b. ¡Qué pronto habéis llegado!

c. Jugábamos con el balón en la playa o íbamos a caminar.

d. ¿De parte de quién?

e. El próximo verano pienso descansar y no hacer nada.

2

Match the sentences on the left with the appropriate reactions on the right.

1. Jordi y yo queremos darte este regalo.

2. ¿A ti te gusta el chile con carne?

3. Oye, Jordi, ¿qué piensas hacer después de las prácticas?

4. Creo que has cogido mi teléfono móvil.

5. Hola, buenos días. Quería hablar con el señor Giménez.

6. ¿Qué tal vuestro viaje por España? ¿Tuvisteis buen tiempo?

a. En Madrid hacía sol, pero hacía bastante frío.

b. Pienso irme de vacaciones.

c. Ah, sí, perdona; pensé que era el mío.

d. ¡Esto sí que no me lo esperaba!

e. ¿Ese plato de carne con frijoles? ¡Me encanta!

f. Un momento, por favor; ahora se pone.

3

First, listen to the dialogue between Charo and Noelia. And you, how do you feel? Are you tired, bored, contented? Can you explain why? Write your answer on another sheet of paper. You will find suggested answers in the companion book.

Stating plans and intentions — Answering questions

4

Complete the sentences by filling in the blanks with the correct verb forms.

> piensa — piensas — va — pensáis — vamos — voy

1. • Y vosotros, ¿qué _____ hacer este fin de semana?

   ○ _____ a visitar a unos amigos.

2. • ¿Adónde _____ irse tu abuela de vacaciones?

   ○ Ella _____ a ir a Benidorm.

3. • ¿Qué _____ hacer después del verano, Rosita?

   ○ Me _____ a trabajar a Barcelona.

5

Read the questions and mark the statement that correctly answers each.

1. ¿Qué vais a hacer hoy?
   a. ▨ Creo que quiere irse a trabajar a Barcelona.
   b. ▨ En abril quiero visitar Sevilla.
   c. ▨ Mi mujer y yo pensamos salir a cenar.

2. ¿Qué hacía ella antes?
   a. ▨ Había un ambiente muy agradable.
   b. ▨ Trabajaba en una empresa internacional.
   c. ▨ Todos los años iban a hacer montañismo.

6

Read and answer the following questions. When you've finished, you can read the suggested answers in the companion book.

1. ¿Qué tiempo hace hoy?
2. De niño, ¿qué hacía usted después del colegio?
3. ¿Desde cuándo vive usted aquí?
4. ¿Qué va a hacer usted mañana?
5. ¿Adónde piensa ir de vacaciones el próximo año?
6. ¿Para qué utiliza usted el ordenador?

Preterit vs. imperfect — The direct object

7 ✏

Look at the verbs in parentheses, which are given in both the preterit and the imperfect tense forms, and write the correct form in each blank.

▶ § 16 Preterit (Indefinido)

▶ § 17 Imperfect

Good to know:
The imperfect tense answers the question *What was it like?* The preterit and the present perfect answer the question *What happened?*

1. ¿Tú no (*diste / dabas*) _____ antes un paseo todos los días?

2. (*estuvimos / estábamos*) _____ cenando tranquilamente, cuando nos lo (*dijeron / decían*) _____ .

3. ¿(*fuisteis / ibais*) _____ al cine ayer por la noche?

4. Cuando era pequeña me (*encantó / encantaba*) _____ ir a la playa.

5. El año pasado (*viajaron / viajaban*) _____ a Cuba.

6. (*hizo / hacía*) _____ tanto frío en la calle que (*decidimos / decidíamos*) _____ regresar.

7. El otro día (*vi / veía*) _____ a Chema hablando con Charo.

8. Él antes (*almorzó / almorzaba*) _____ en la cantina de la empresa.

8 ✏

Complete the passage by filling in the blanks with the correct forms. You won't need to use all the words given!

estábamos — quisimos — íbamos — propuso — estuvimos — fue — queríamos — fuimos — era — proponía

_____ tardísimo, todos _____ muy cansados y

_____ irnos a casa. _____ a tomar un taxi, cuando entonces

Rosita, de repente, _____ ir a desayunar chocolate con churros …

9 ✏

In the sentences below, add the preposition **a** wherever necessary.

▶ § 31 Direct Object

1. Estamos buscando _____ el Museo Reina Sofía.

2. Voy a llamar _____ la agencia de viajes.

3. ¿Habéis visto _____ Rosita en el restaurante?

*Prepositions of time — Direct object pronouns — **seguir** + present participle — **ser** and **estar***

10 ✎

▶ § 37 Prepositions

Do you remember the following expressions?

hace + period of time = *ago*
desde + period of time = *since*
desde hace + period of time = *for*

Complete the following sentences with the appropriate expressions.

1. Chema y Noelia están en México _____ el jueves pasado.

2. Los chicos se conocen _____ mucho tiempo.

3. Mi mujer y yo estuvimos en Sevilla _____ un par de semanas.

11 ✎

▶ § 26 Direct Object Pronouns

Complete the sentences with the correct direct object pronouns.

1. Esos libros, se _____ he regalado yo.

2. Esta lechuga, ¿_____ has comprado en el supermercado?

3. Las chuletas, _____ preparan muy bien en Casa Pancho.

4. A Agustín, no _____ hemos visto hoy.

12 ✎

▶ § 18 Present Participle

Complete the sentences below with the appropriate forms of the verb **seguir.**

1. ¿ _____ trabajando en la misma empresa, Jordi?

2. Pero, chicos, ¿todavía _____ buscando vuelos a México?

3. Yo _____ viviendo en esta calle, pero ahora en el número 3.

13 ✎

▶ § 19 ser / estar

Complete the following sentences by using the verbs **ser** and **estar**.

1. Mi marido _____ muy activo; siempre está haciendo algo.

2. Hoy _____ muy amable conmigo. A ver, ¿qué me quieres pedir?

3. Los chicos _____ muy contentos porque por fin han encontrado un vuelo.

The months — The weather

14 ✏️

Do you remember the names of the months? Write the missing ones in the blanks.

Los meses del año son:

enero, _____, marzo,

abril, mayo, _____,

_____, _____, septiembre,

_____, noviembre y diciembre.

15 ✏️

Match the sentences below with the correct pictures. You'll have a few expressions left over!

1.

2.

3.

4.

5.

a. Llueve mucho. — b. Hace mucho frío. — c. Nieva. — d. Está nublado. —
e. Hay niebla. — f. Hace sol. — g. Hace viento. — h. Hace calor.

16 ✏️

Look at the pictures and complete each expression with the missing word.

1. Hace

_____.

2. Hay

_____.

3. Está

_____.

4. Hace

_____.

Feelings and moods — Finding words

17

Look at the pictures. Which words go with which pictures?

1. Jordi está	2. Noelia está	3. Agustín está
a. ▪ enfermo.	a. ▪ triste.	a. ▪ agotado.
b. ▪ nervioso.	b. ▪ contenta.	b. ▪ enfadado.
c. ▪ aburrido.	c. ▪ preocupada.	c. ▪ triste.

18

The words we're looking for all have to do with the topic of "language courses." Put the letters in the right order. For nouns, the strings of letters also include the definite articles.

1. luracalaímt   2. adnerper   3. eimaolldp

_____   _____   _____

19

For each category, find the word that doesn't go with the others, and mark it.

1.	2.	3.	4.
cuñado	rojo	alfombra	agradable
hermana	mosto	silla	collar
nieto	refresco	sangría	sincero
bombero	zumo	estantería	tímida

5.	6.	7.	8.
agenda	fotógrafo	merluza	marido
balcón	abierto	albóndigas	cebolla
cartera	profesor	bacalao	arroz
gafas	médica	furgoneta	harina

Travel vocabulary — A postcard from Yucatán

20

Read the following questions and mark the correct answers.

1. ¿Qué pueblo vivía en el centro de México?

   a. ▨ los incas
   b. ▨ los aztecas
   c. ▨ los mayas

2. ¿Qué ciudad de los mayas está situada en la costa de Yucatán?

   a. ▨ Tulúm
   b. ▨ Chichén-Itzá
   c. ▨ Uxmal

◀ **el pueblo** — *people*
la costa — *coast*
situado / a —
situated, located

21

How do you say these words in Spanish? Write down the Spanish terms with their appropriate definite articles (**el** or **la**).

1. stay — 2. trip — 3. ticket — 4. flight — 5. lodgings, accommodations

22

Complete the postcard Noelia is writing to her family. In some cases, there are several possible answers.

¡Hola, familia!

¡Por _____ estamos en Yucatán! El viaje de Madrid a Mérida

_____ un poco largo, pero muy divertido.

Nuestro _____ es muy bonito. Está en la parte antigua de la

_____ . Tiene restaurante y también una pequeña piscina.

Ayer _____ Uxmal, uno de los centros arqueológicos más impor-

tantes de Yucatán. A Chema y a mí _____ gustó mucho.

Mañana _____ a visitar Chichén-Itzá y después pensamos

_____ a Tulúm.

Un beso, Noelia y Chema

Elision — Mexican dishes

23

As you are already aware, the words in a Spanish sentence are blended together in a process called "elision." This process also occurs when a word begins with the letter **h**, since this consonant is silent.

Listen to the following sentences, paying attention to the linking or omission of sounds. Then repeat the sentences.

> Vamos a seguir buscando, a ver si encontramos algo …
>
> Yo no conozco a esas amigas tuyas.
>
> Le ofrecemos las mejores ofertas de viaje.
>
> A ella le encanta navegar por internet.

24

Using the CD, listen to the descriptions of four Mexican dishes, and match them with the names of the dishes below.

1.   a. Pozole

2.   b. Quesadilla

3.   c. Mole

4.   d. Enchilada

Photo sources:

Page 18   Eduard Bader, Esslingen (*Two people greeting each other*)

Page 26   Klaus Thiele, Warburg (*Plaza Real, Madrid*)

Page 26   Spanish Tourist Office, Munich (*El Rastro, Madrid*)

Page 26   Magdalena Witkowski (*Puerta del Sol, Madrid*)

Page 26   Magdalena Witkowski (*Museo de Arte Moderno Reina Sofía, Madrid*)

Page 34, Page 49 Andrea Laufer-Newcomb, Böblingen (*Zócalo with the Cathedral in Mexico City*)

Page 34   Mexican Tourist Office, Frankfurt/Main (*Pirámide, México*)

Page 58   Eduard Bader, Esslingen (*Two people on the street*)

Page 74   EKS GmbH, Stuttgart (*Calling card*)

Page 89   EKS GmbH, Stuttgart (*Retiro, Madrid*)

Page 98   EKS GmbH, Stuttgart (*Making a tortilla*)

Page 98   EKS GmbH, Stuttgart (*Tortilla española*)

Page 98   EKS GmbH, Stuttgart (*Mexican dish*)

Page 106   University of Kentucky, Lexington (*In a tapería*)

Page 106   University of Kentucky, Lexington (*People eating tapas*)

Page 115   EKS GmbH, Stuttgart (*Menu*)

Page 122   Roger Gill, Tübingen (*In a restaurant*)

Page 129   EKS GmbH, Stuttgart (*Catedral Nueva de Salamanca*)

Page 138   Eduard Bader, Esslingen (*Terraza, Madrid*)

Page 138   University of Kentucky, Lexington (*Churros con chocolate, a Spanish specialty*)

Page 146   Getty Images, Munich (*Corn*)

Page 154   EKS GmbH, Stuttgart (*Lottery tickets, Spain*)

Page 162   Mexican Tourist Office, Frankfurt/Main (*Ruinas de Tulum, México*)

Page 162   Dominique Nißler, Stuttgart (*Mérida, México*)

Page 169   Dominique Nißler, Stuttgart (*Ruinas Mayas de Uxmal, México*)

Recording, editing, and mastering:
Ton in Ton Medienhaus, Stuttgart

Editing:
ARTist Tonstudios, Pfullingen

Speakers:
María Begoña Abaitua de Nägele
Svetlana Pavlovic López
Beatriz Eugenia Alba de Berger
Susanne Schmitz
Elena Alvarez
Enrique Ugarte
José Cadiñanos
Mónica Cociña Iglesias
Cristóbal Delgado Cervera
Miguel Freire Gómez
María Engracia López Sánchez
Carlos Ortega

AT A GLANCE Series

Barron's new series gives travelers instant access to the most common idiomatic expressions used during a trip—the kind one needs to know instantly, like "Where can I find a taxi?" and "How much does this cost?"

Organized by situation (arrival, customs, hotel, health, etc.) and containing additional information about pronunciation, grammar, shopping plus special facts about the country, these convenient, pocket-size reference books will be the tourist's most helpful guides.

Special features include a bilingual dictionary section with over 2000 key words, maps of each country and major cities, and helpful phonetic spellings throughout.

Each book paperback, 256 pp., 3 3/4" × 6"

ARABIC AT A GLANCE, Wise (0-7641-1248-1) $8.95, Can. $12.50
CHINESE AT A GLANCE, Seligman & Chen (0-7641-1250-3) $8.95, Can. $12.50
FRENCH AT A GLANCE, 4th, Stein & Wald (0-7641-2512-5) $6.95, Can. $9.95
GERMAN AT A GLANCE, 4th, Strutz (0-7641-2516-8) $6.95, Can. $9.95
ITALIAN AT A GLANCE, 4th, Costantino (0-7641-2513-3) $6.95, Can. $9.95
JAPANESE AT A GLANCE, 3rd, Akiyama (0-7641-0320-2) $8.95, Can. $11.95
KOREAN AT A GLANCE, Holt (0-8120-3998-X) $8.95, Can. $11.95
RUSSIAN AT A GLANCE, Beyer (0-7641-1251-1) $8.95, Can. $12.50
SPANISH AT A GLANCE, 4th, Wald (0-7641-2514-1) $6.95, Can. $9.95

Barron's Educational Series, Inc.
250 Wireless Blvd., Hauppauge, NY 11788
Call toll-free: 1-800-645-3476
In Canada: Georgetown Book Warehouse, 34 Armstrong Ave.
Georgetown, Ont. L7G 4R9, Call toll-free: 1-800-247-7160
Visit our website at: www.barronseduc.com

Books may be purchased at your bookstore, or by mail from Barron's. Enclose check or money order for total amount plus sales tax where applicable and 18% for postage and handling (minimum charge $5.95). New York, New Jersey, Michigan, and California residents add sales tax. Prices subject to change without notice.
Can. $ = Canadian dollars

(#25) R 11/05

Helpful Guides for Mastering a Foreign Language

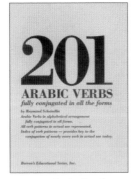

2001 Idiom Series

Indispensable resources, these completely bilingual dictionaries in four major European languages present the most frequently used idiomatic words and phrases to help students avoid stilted expression when writing in their newly acquired language. Each book includes illustrative sentences. Each feature is easy to locate and designed with clarity in mind.

2001 French and English Idioms, 2nd
0-8120-9024-1 $16.95, Can $23.95

2001 German and English Idioms
0-8120-9009-8 $16.95, Can $23.95

2001 Italian and English Idioms
0-8120-9030-6 $18.99, Can $27.50

2001 Japanese and English Idioms
0-8120-9433-6 $18.99, Can $27.50

2001 Russian and English Idioms
0-8120-9532-4 $21.95, Can $31.95

2001 Spanish and English Idioms
0-8120-9028-4 $16.99, Can $24.50

201 Verb Series

The most commonly used verbs are presented alphabetically and in all their forms, one to a page, in each of the many foreign languages listed here. Features of this series include discussions of participles, punctuation guides, listings of compounds, the phrases and expressions often used with each verb, plus much more!

201 Arabic Verbs
0-8120-0547-3 $14.99, Can $21.99

201 Dutch Verbs
0-8120-0738-7 $14.95, Can $21.95

201 Modern Greek Verbs
0-8120-0475-2 $14.995, Can $21.99

201 Polish Verbs
0-7641-1029-9 $16.95, Can $24.50

201 Swedish Verbs
0-8120-0528-7 $16.95, Can $24.50

201 Turkish Verbs
0-8120-2034-0 $14.95, Can $21.00

501 Verb Series

Here is a series to help the foreign language student successfully approach verbs and all their details. Complete conjugations of the verbs are arranged one verb to a page in alphabetical order. Verb forms are printed in boldface type in two columns, and common idioms using the applicable verbs are listed at the bottom of the page in each volume.

501 English Verbs
0-7641-0304-0 $14.95, Can $19.95

501 French Verbs, 4th
0-7641-2429-3 $14.95, Can $21.95

501 German Verbs, 3rd
0-7641-0284-2 $14.95, Can $19.95

501 Hebrew Verbs
0-8120-9468-9 $18.95, Can $27.50

501 Italian Verbs
0-7641-1348-8 $14.95, Can $21.00

501 Japanese Verbs, 2nd
0-7641-0285-0 $16.95, Can $23.95

501 Latin Verbs
0-8120-9050-9 $18.99, Can $27.50

501 Portuguese Verbs, 2nd
0-7641-2916-3 $16.95, Can $24.50

501 Russian Verbs
0-7641-1349-6 $16.95, Can $24.50

501 Spanish Verbs, 4th
0-7641-2428-5 $14.95, Can $21.00

Barron's Educational Series, Inc. •
250 Wireless Boulevard,
Hauppauge, NY 11788
Call toll-free: 1-800-645-3476

In Canada:
Georgetown Book Warehouse
34 Armstrong Avenue, Georgetown,
Ont. L7G 4R9
Call toll-free: 1-800-247-7160

(#33) R 11/05

3 Foreign Language Series From Barron's!

The **VERB SERIES** offers more than 300 of the most frequently used verbs.
The **GRAMMAR SERIES** provides complete coverage of the elements of grammar.
The **VOCABULARY SERIES** offers more than 3500 words and phrases with their foreign language translations.
Each book: paperback.

Barron's Educational Series, Inc.
250 Wireless Blvd., Hauppauge, NY 11788
Call toll-free: 1-800-645-3476
In Canada: Georgetown Book Warehouse
34 Armstrong Ave., Georgetown, Ontario L7G 4R9
Call toll-free: 1-800-247-7160
www.barronseduc.com
Can. $ = Canadian dollars

Books may be purchased at your bookstore or by mail from Barron's. Enclose check or money order for total amount plus sales tax where applicable and 18% for postage and handling (minimum charge $5.95 U.S. and Canada). Prices subject to change without notice. New York, New Jersey, Michigan, and California residents, please add sales tax to total after postage and handling.

(#26) R 11/05

Notes